TWENTIETH CENTURY INTERPRETATIONS
OF
TO THE LIGHTHOUSE

TWENTIETH CENTURY
INTERPRETATIONS
OF
TO THE
LIGHTHOUSE

A Collection of Critical Essays

Edited by

THOMAS A. VOGLER

Prentice-Hall, Inc. *Englewood Cliffs, N. J.*

A SPECTRUM BOOK

Copyright © 1970 by Prentice-Hall, Inc., Englewood Cliffs, New Jersey. A SPEC-
TRUM BOOK. All rights reserved. No part of this book may be reproduced in any
form or by any means without permission in writing from the publisher. C–13-
923227-3; P–13-923219-2. *Library of Congress Catalog Card Number 79–120798.*
Printed in the United States of America.

Current printing (last number):
10 9 8 7 6 5 4 3 2 1

PRENTICE-HALL INTERNATIONAL, INC. (*London*)
PRENTICE-HALL OF AUSTRALIA, PTY. LTD. (*Sydney*)
PRENTICE-HALL OF CANADA, LTD. (*Toronto*)
PRENTICE-HALL OF INDIA PRIVATE LIMITED (*New Delhi*)
PRENTICE-HALL OF JAPAN, INC. (*Tokyo*)

Contents

TWENTIETH CENTURY INTERPRETATIONS
OF
TO THE LIGHTHOUSE

Introduction

Adeline Virginia Stephen was born on January 25, 1882 at Hyde Park Gate, Kensington. Her father, Leslie Stephen, had been a Cambridge don until 1864, when he left for religious reasons centering in his agnosticism. He remained an active force in the English world of letters, however, as an editor, critic, journalist, and biographer who published almost forty works during his lifetime. Virginia's mother, Julia Duckworth, was Leslie Stephen's second wife. At the time of their marriage she was a widow with three children, so that with their four (Virginia, Vanessa, Thoby, and Adrian) plus a daughter by Leslie Stephen's first marriage, the household numbered eight children.

In 1881 Leslie Stephen had bought a house at St. Ives in Cornwall, where the family went for summer vacations each year until Julia Stephen's death in 1895. Although a formidable figure in the public realm, Virginia's father committed much of his time and energies to his family. In her essay on him ("Leslie Stephen," *The Captain's Death Bed*) she describes his reading the Waverley Novels to the children, and spending Sundays reciting the many poems he knew by heart. He also had time to take her on long walks through the streets of London, a favorite pastime for them both. Her health was not up to a formal education, so she was tutored at home and given free access to her father's library, which had a large and representative collection of the classics and the best English literature. She later remembered the library as one of her favorite places, and the source of her inspiration for her first writing.

After her father's death in 1904 she lived with her sister Vanessa at 46 Gordon Square, Bloomsbury, and began her career as a writer. She wrote mainly reviews and essays at first, many of which appeared anonymously in the *Times Literary Supplement*. She started her first novel (*The Voyage Out*) in 1906, took seven years to finish it, and two more to publish it. Meanwhile, her sister Vanessa had married Clive Bell and Virginia moved with her brother Adrian to a different house in Bloomsbury. It was during this period that the famous "Bloomsbury Group" began with a nucleus of Cambridge friends that was soon to include most of the London intellectual aristocracy.

In 1912 she married Leonard Woolf, a man of many interests and talents who was earning a significant reputation as a political thinker and essayist. Together they founded the Hogarth Press in 1917, printing books on a small hand press in Hogarth House, 34 Paradise Road, Richmond-on-Thames. In addition to the Woolfs' works, they published T. S. Eliot's *Poems* (1919) and a small but steady stream of important and interesting books. As the press grew from a hobby to a full-scale publishing business, much of Virginia Woolf's time was spent in reading, editing, and publishing works for the press, as well as continuing her own writing of essays and fiction, and engaging in discussions with the most important thinkers and writers of her time. Eliot, who was a peripheral member of the Bloomsbury Group, has written that

> Virginia Woolf was the centre, not merely of an esoteric group, but of the literary life of London. Her position was due to a concurrence of qualities and circumstances which never happened before, and which I do not think will ever happen again. (*Horizon*, May, 1941)

She wrote nine novels in all, from *The Voyage Out* to *Between the Acts,* which was completed but unrevised at the time of her death. Her writing career was followed closely through the twenties and thirties, each novel receiving mixed reviews. Her work was consistently experimental, so that *Mrs. Dalloway* (1925) and *To the Lighthouse* (1927) became known as her best work, while the later novels, largely because of their differences and idosyncrasies of form, and the changing temper of the thirties, were commonly held to be a falling off. Work itself seems to have been a necessity for her. The *Diary* records, after the completion of each novel, an inevitable period of despondency and self-doubt which could only be eased by starting a new work or by reading and annotating countless manuscripts for the press.

It may be that the *Diary,* edited by Leonard Woolf from the twenty-six volumes filled between 1915 and 1941, is not fully representative of her inner life. Woolf's criteria were based on those parts of the journal which related most closely to her writing, and she herself commented that "I only record the dumps and the dismals and them very barely." (Feb. 28, 1939) Friends remembered her as being gay and vivacious. Works like *Orlando* and *Flush* (a biography of Elizabeth Browning's dog) combine a capacity for humor with a genuine gift of wit. Yet the *Diary* does reflect that inner sense of quiet desperation against which she pitted her life and her work.

She lived much of her life with a recurring fear of insanity after her breakdown during World War I, and suicide was often in her mind as a last resort against the ultimate catastrophes of life. In March,

1941, having finished *Between the Acts,* exhausted by the writing and doubtful of its value, having had her London home and library destroyed in air raids, she went out for her usual walk across South Downs and drowned herself in the River Ouse. Although her death was widely attributed to despair over the war and the possibility of a German victory, her notes to her sister and Leonard Woolf make it clear that she could finally fight her inner darkness no longer:

> I have the feeling that I shall go mad. I hear voices and cannot concentrate on my work. I have fought against it, but cannot fight any longer. I owe all my happiness in life to you. You have been so perfectly good. I cannot go and spoil your life.

Backgrounds

> But meanwhile, while we eat, let us turn over these scenes as children turn over the pages of a picture-book and the nurse says, pointing: "That's a cow. That's a boat." Let us turn over the pages, and I will add, for your amusement, a comment in the margin. (Bernard in *The Waves*)

Much of Virginia Woolf's work, as well as her life, is rooted in the "spirit of the age" that pervaded the early twentieth century. She read almost everything, and kept up eagerly with all the art movements in England and on the continent. Without arguing influence one way or the other, it is a good idea to have some sense of the intellectual and artistic atmosphere of the period that she lived through and wrote in. A main feature of most writers and artists during this period was a self-conscious insistence on experimental forms and on "making it new" or seeing it for the first time. In art this urge gave rise to numerous new schools and manifestos of artistic principles: Cubism, Dadism, Purism, Neoplasticism, Constructivism, Orphism, Vorticism, Fantasism, Abstractionism, Surrealism, as well as the more familiar Impressionism and Expressionism. In literature, the Imagists were everywhere, and the "stream of consciousness" (William James' phrase), as well as Freud and Bergson, was being explored for possible implication. As a novelist Virginia Woolf shared the ferment: "I have an idea," she wrote while working on *To the Lighthouse,* "that I will invent a new name for my books to supplant 'novel.' A new ——— by Virginia Woolf. But what? Elegy?" [1] But she also shared the negative implications of the search for new forms; the

---

[1] *A Writer's Diary: Being Extracts from the Diary of Virginia Woolf,* ed. Leonard Woolf (London: Hogarth Press, 1969), entry for June 27, 1925, p. 80. Future references to the *Diary* will give only date and page number.

old were no longer available or relevant either to art or life. The surface of things was gone, and with it representative and conscious modes of form; some other form must be found, or the possibilities of form denied altogether. Several features of this ferment need to be isolated for closer view before we go on to *To the Lighthouse*.

The importance of the visual arts for the whole movement, and for Virginia Woolf in particular, was tied to a growing sense of limitation in the traditional use of words as an artistic medium. In the eighteenth century Lessing had taken among his "first principles" the view that "painting employs wholly different signs or means of imitation from poetry,—the one using forms and colors in space, the other articulate sounds in time," and that "signs arranged side by side can represent only objects existing side by side . . . while consecutive signs can express only objects which succeed each other, in time." [2] These traditional "limitations" on their medium were intolerable to writers who saw the temporal implications of the painting movements; the painters were going beyond representational service to the side-by-side and conscious aspect of vision—fragmenting, presenting an "instant" of vision based on non-visual data, juxtaposing arbitrary, evocative and untranslatable images, and ignoring their "limitations." The poets envied the painters their medium which admitted the simultaneous exploration of vision and space and the possibilities of "pure" form in abstractions. Some, like Apollinaire, Dos Passos, and Cummings, tried for visual or graphic effects, but all sought for an alternative to the constricting view that words were an inherently linear and time-bound medium.

This constriction was not being resisted for the sake of novelty alone, but as part of the struggle to keep literature abreast of the new ideas about the way human consciousness exists in time, and makes contact with whatever reality exists outside itself:

> . . . the cosmic objects, so far as the experience yields them, are but ideal pictures of something whose existence we do not inwardly possess but only point 'at outwardly, while the inner state is our very experience itself; its reality and that of our experience are one . . . such a concrete bit of personal experience may be a small bit, but it is a solid bit as long as it lasts . . . it is of the *kind* to which all realities whatsoever must belong. . . .

> A bill of fare with one real raisin on it instead of the word "raisin," with one real egg instead of the word "egg," might be an inadequate meal, but it would at least be a commencement of reality.[3]

[2] *Laocoon: An Essay Upon the Limits of Painting and Poetry*, trans. Ellen Frothingham (New York: Farrar, Straus & Giroux, Inc., 1965), p. 91.

[3] William James, *Varieties of Religious Experience* (New York: University Books, Inc., 1963), pp. 499–500. First published in 1902.

Bergson's attempt to break up the conception of the world as machine, surface, and material, in his speculations on time and memory, was a counterpart to and an influence on the experimentation in art. His notions of time as fluid and always in motion, of memory as constantly pressing in on the present, and of space as the more "manageable" dimension, are contained in his theory of human time as a *durée*. The Bergsonian *durée* is psychological time as opposed to clock time; it is constituted in the streamy flux of the subjective world and, like Mrs. Ramsay, knows "objects" through intuition as internal states rather than from outside as objects.

If consciousness is the touchstone of "knowable" reality, and consciousness has no absolute linear existence in time, then the literary work must ignore or destroy conventional time as a primary principle of artistic form. Pound, speaking for the Imagists, set his goal as

> . . . the presentation of such a complex [consciousness in an instant of time] which gives that sense of sudden liberation; that sense of freedom from time limits and space limits; that sense of sudden growth, which we experience in the presence of great works of art.[4]

Virginia Woolf had a similar problem and goal in her mind while working on *To the Lighthouse:*

> I am now and then haunted by some semi-mystic very profound life of a woman, which shall all be told on one occasion; and time shall be utterly obliterated; future shall somehow blossom out of the past. One incident—say the fall of a flower—might contain it. My theory being that the actual event practically does not exist—nor time either. (Nov. 23, 1926, p. 102)

This goal is reflected also in Proust's notion of the *moment privilégié*, and in the general tendency of novels of whatever size to focus down on narrower and narrower dimensions in linear time, and to ignore the convention linearity in their presentations of those "spots of time" within the narrow focus. For, as these spots become isolated, they partake of that same "relativity" in the theoretical work of Einstein that denies the Newtonian absolutes of space and time.

As these moments of consciousness were explored by writers, they began to make on their own many of the discoveries about the multiplicity of levels present in a single experience that are often attributed to Freud. The human instinct can urge both life and death simultaneously, and love and hate can be simultaneous components of a relationship or attitude. "Feelings which used to come single and

[4] "A Few Don'ts by an Imagiste," *Poetry* (March, 1913); included in "A Retrospect," *Pavannes and Divisions* (New York: Alfred A. Knopf, Inc., 1918), pp. 95–111.

separate do so no longer. Beauty is part ugliness; amusement part disgust; pleasure part pain." [5] Even more complex is the discovery that some components of an experience may be in consciousness but not raised to the conscious level. They too must be included:

> What is my own position towards the inner and the outer? . . . to give the moment whole; whatever it includes. Say that the moment is a combination of thought; sensation; the voice of the sea . . . a match burning in a crocus, an inner meaning almost expressed. . . . (Nov. 28, 1928, p. 138)

And if the point is true of experience generally, it must be there— and accounted for—in the experience of creating a work of art. ". . . how tremendously important unconsciousness is when one writes," he exclaimed at one point in the *Diary* (Oct. 29, 1933, p. 213).

Along with these emphases, and also "modern," is her incorporation of the artist's consciousness and creative perception into the work in an attempt to fuse life and art. For life to be bearable or real, it must have the sense of form which we call "identity" on the individual level. For art to be significant (by being "real") it must have the felt quality of life in its full intensity:

> All art, therefore, appeals primarily to the senses, and the artistic aim when expressing itself in written words must also make its appeal through the senses, if its high desire is to reach the secret spring of responsive emotions.[6]

To achieve both the form and the feeling of life, a story cannot propose as real a structure based on time with a conventional beginning and end. The story must surround life all at once as a "luminous halo":

> Examine for a moment an ordinary mind on an ordinary day. The mind receives a myriad impressions—trivial, fantastic, evanescent, or engraved with the sharpness of steel. From all sides they come, an incessant shower of innumerable atoms; and as they fall, as they shape themselves into the life of Monday or Tuesday, the accent falls differently from of old; the moment of importance came not here but there; so that, if a writer were a free man and not a slave, if he could write what he chose, not what he must, if he could base his work upon his own feeling and not upon convention, there would be no plot, no comedy, no tragedy, no love interest or catastrophe in the accepted style, and perhaps not a single button sewn on as the Bond Street tailors would have it. Life is not a series of gig-lamps symmetrically arranged; life is a luminous halo, a semi-

---

[5] "The Narrow Bridge of Art," *Granite and Rainbow* (New York: Harcourt, Brace, 1958) p. 16.

[6] Conrad, Preface to *The Nigger of the Narcissus* (New York: Doubleday & Company, Inc., 1960), p. xiii.

transparent envelope surrounding us from the beginning of consciousness to the end. Is it not the task of the novelist to convey this varying, this unknown and uncircumscribed spirit, whatever aberration or complexity it may display, with as little mixture of the alien and external as possible? [7]

Her image in this, as well as her goal, is strikingly similar to that of Conrad's Marlow in *Heart of Darkness:*

> The yarns of seamen have a direct simplicity, the whole meaning of which lies within the shell of a cracked nut. But Marlow was not typical . . . and to him the meaning of an episode was not inside like a kernel but outside, enveloping the tale which brought it out only as a glow brings out a haze, in the likeness of one of these misty halos that sometimes are made visible by the spectral illumination of moonshine.

In his Preface to *The Ambassadors,* James points out that "There is the story of one's hero, and then, thanks to the intimate connection of things, the story of one's story itself." While James chose to separate the story of his stories in his *Prefaces,* Virginia Woolf chose to include the "story" of creating *To the Lighthouse* in the novel itself. By having Lily Briscoe be a painter suspicious of words rather than a writer, she avoids some of the problems while achieving the same goal as Conrad in his Marlow stories, Cervantes in *Don Quixote,* Brontë in *Wuthering Heights,* Melville in *Moby Dick* and *Pierre,* Proust in *A la Recherche du Temps Perdu,* Fitzgerald in *The Great Gatsby,* Nabokov in *Pale Fire, Sebastien Knight,* and others, Ellison in *Invisible Man,* and numerous other novelists of the last 100 years. The goal is to include the creation or telling of the story in the story itself, as an element so important that it tends to supplant the more conventional notion of "story" as the main focus of the work. The use of double characters, one rooted in life (and death), the other in art, is also a common feature she shares with many other novelists. In this mode the "life" character (like Mrs. Ramsay) lives or represents the human reality of the story, and the narrator or observer (Lily Briscoe) tries to get at the form and essence of the story through art. This is most obvious when the "life" character dies and we discover that the artist and his experience have been the central concern all along, that his commitment to form and meaning (rather than the other's commitment to action) is the real clue to whatever significance life may have.

One final point about the "spirit of the times" may be worth making, before we turn to the novel. In this period *none* of the great writers were Religious, and *all* of them were religious. They wrote about religious problems and religion itself, they shared a "religious" feeling for the value of life, but in such a way that Religion in its conventional

[7] *Collected Essays* (New York: Harcourt, Brace & World, Inc., 1967), p. 106.

sense became part of that larger life that was their subject. Whether we call it secularism or humanism, or humanist secularism, it is a predominant attitude of the times, and must be distinguished from the concept of "atheism" that was totally alien to it. Leslie Stephen, in his militant agnosticism, fell into a psychological dogmatism precisely like that Religion against which he was rebelling. Virginia Woolf was able to hold the question of the existence of God in abeyance in all her work, and yet to feel that if He did exist she was writing about Him. When Mrs. Ramsay says, "We are in the hands of God," she herself does not know what it means, and for the novelist it is a part of Mrs. Ramsay's character that must be presented.[8]

To the Lighthouse

The works I have chosen for this collection represent a number of important approaches to the novel; they should be read as beginnings that will repay careful thought and following up. Without attempting anything like a full interpretation, I would like to introduce them by making a number of suggestions and warnings that can be found from a careful reading of the novel itself. The categories I have chosen are inevitably arbitrary, and the order I present them in is irrelevant—any one, if pursued, soon leads to another because of the organic and fluid qualities of the novel.

BIOGRAPHY

And this, Lily thought, taking the green paint on her brush, this making up scenes about them, is what we call "knowing" people, "thinking" of them, "being fond" of them! Not a word of it was true; she had made it up; but it was what she knew them by all the same.

It is clear that there are many connections between the novel and Virginia Woolf's own life, and that the majority of these connections are from her period of growing up. The Stephen family was intellectually distinguished, like the Ramsays, and spent its summers, as earlier noted, in a Cornwall setting very much like the Skye of the novel, where eight children throve. Virginia Woolf's great-grandmother was French, and Mrs. Ramsay proudly announces that the *Boeuf en Daube* is "a French recipe of my grandmother's"; her

---

[8] One would think this point unnecessary were it not for those who praise or condemn her for being an "atheist," and for those who read the novel as "an allegory . . . based principally on the Bible." (F. L. Overcarsh, "The Lighthouse, Face to Face," *Accent* [Winter, 1950], pp. 107–23.)

brother Thoby died quite suddenly in Greece, as Andrew dies in the war—there are innumerable details of this sort that might creep into any writer's work based on the experience of his own life. It is when we try to go from the details to the characters themselves, and to the larger sense in which Virginia Woolf was basing the novel on herself and her family that we run into problems. The tendency is to assume that we know how she felt about her parents and early life and to find that knowledge reflected in the novel, without realizing that the relationship works both ways—that the novel, from the perspective of time, is the opportunity for Virginia Woolf to work through and discover for herself who her parents were and how she felt about them. To say, as Leavis does, that

> The substance of this novel was provided directly by life. . . . We know enough about Leslie Stephen . . . and his family to know that there is a large measure of direct transcription. We can see a clear connection between this fact and the unique success of *To the Lighthouse* among her novels.[9]

is to miss the whole level of creative exploration of the past that is revealed in every facet of the novel. To "know" the character of Leslie Stephen, and to know Virginia Woolf's attitude towards him are two different things, and the novel (together with the *Diary*) is our only way to discover the latter.

The most important reason for setting the novel in a fictional world similar to the real St. Ives is not transcription of detail, but the double isolation (in time and space) that Virginia Woolf needed to explore her attitudes towards herself and her family. They spent most of their time in London; but as a family, constituting the narrower world of a growing child, they could be seen more clearly in Cornwall separated from their other competing interests and identities. In one of her earliest entries mentioning *To the Lighthouse*, she wrote:

> . . . get on to *To the Lighthouse*. This is going to be fairly short; to have father's character done complete in it; and mother's; and St. Ives; and childhood; and all the usual things I try to put in—life, death, etc. But the centre is father's character, sitting in a boat, reciting We perished, each alone, while he crushes a dying mackerel. (May 14, 1925, pp. 76–77)

Mr. Ramsay did not turn out to be the "centre" of the novel in this original sense, and the mackerel's "mutilated body (it was alive still)" is allowed to return to the sea. It is clear that Lily's adding the final line to her painting at the end is—among other things—a reflection of the clarification of Mr. Ramsay that is going on in Part III. Lily's

---

[9] *Scrutiny* 10, no. 3 (1942): 297.

painting in Part I had been a dark triangle representing Mrs. Ramsay and James, with Mr. Ramsay actually interfering with the work. In III his presence is crucial (though Lily is thankful for the "distance" between her and the boat), as the *Diary* entry anticipated.

As a man, Leslie Stephen had negative feelings about "creative writing," which must have been difficult for Virginia Woolf to live with, creating much the same uneasiness Lily feels about Mr. Ramsay looking at her painting. He feared that his books would not last, as Mr. Ramsay does; he was temperamental and irascible, with strong views on almost everything; he walked constantly, recited poetry, and was very much concerned with his own family and the family itself as an institution.[10] But this does not tell us what Virginia Woolf felt about him as a child, or how she remembered him after he died. The diary reveals extremely intense feelings of having been threatened by him in some profound way:

> Father's birthday. He would have been 96, 96, yes, today; and could have been 96, like other people one has known: but mercifully was not. His life would have entirely ended mine. What would have happened? No writing, no books;—inconceivable.

And a continuation suggests that the writing of *To the Lighthouse* was a way of structuring her memories so that she could live with them:

> I used to think of him and mother daily; but writing *The Lighthouse* laid them in my mind. And now he comes back sometimes, but differently. (I believe this to be true—that I was obsessed by them both, unhealthily; and writing of them was a necessary act.) He comes back now more as a contemporary. I must read him someday. (Nov. 28, 1928, p. 138)

We can trace some of the workings of this "necessary act" by looking at the novel from the biographical point of view. The first part centers on Mrs. Ramsay, rather than Mr. Ramsay. Throughout Part I, Lily is working on her painting of Mrs. Ramsay or working it out on the tablecloth at dinner. Lily is a reflection of Virginia Woolf the artist, exploring and creating the character of Mrs. Ramsay as a person and a mother. Lily is an artist *manqué;* she is "skimpy" in Mr. Ramsay's eyes, virginal and pure (as her name suggests) even though she is thirty-three. The attitude of awe and admiration that Lily has for Mrs. Ramsay, and her feelings of inadequacy (cf. her daubings and the mighty *Boeuf en Daube!*) reflect both the daughter's feelings for

---

[10] In his *Science of Ethics* (New York: G. P. Putnam's Sons, 1882) he founded the "moral health" of society on achieving the proper harmony and values in family life.

an extremely feminine mother and the artist's feelings that art is in some vital way inferior to life. "But all this seemed so little, so virginal, against the other."

At the end of Part I Mr. Ramsay and Mrs. Ramsay are alone together. "He wanted something—wanted the thing she always found it so difficult to give him; wanted her to tell him that she loved him." She will not say it directly, for "she never could say what she felt." Instead, she smiles and triumphs for "She had not said it: yet he knew." At the end of Part III Lily, who distrusts words too, has a comparable moment of triumph:

> . . . the effort of looking at it and the effort of thinking of him landing there, which both seemed to be one and the same effort, had stretched her body and mind to the utmost. Ah, but she was relieved. Whatever she had wanted to give him, when he left her that morning, she had given him at last.

Structurally, the echo adds a bit of symmetry that reflects the formal subtlety of the novel. But psychologically, it suggests how Virginia Woolf, as daughter and writer, can still give her father something, even though it is not the gift of the mother whose art is life itself.

The gap between Parts I and III is ten years, and there are many artistic and philosophical reasons for the jump. In the present context, however, it should be emphasized that the time covered is the span of a child's growing up. Lily is now 44, the age of Woolf when she finished the novel. Cam, on the other hand, is about 15 or 16 as she rides passively out to the Lighthouse, resenting every minute of it. Although Cam tends to weave fragmentary stories out of her experience as it happens, she is more clearly the "daughter-figure" in this part of the novel. Mr. Ramsay repeats with her (over the points of the compass) his angry outburst with Mrs. Ramsay over the weather, and she feels a complex mixture of desire ("For no one attracted her more.") and repulsion ("that crass blindness and tyranny of his which had poisoned her childhood and raised bitter storms"), neither of which represents a final perception of her father:

> . . . for she was thinking, as the boat sailed on, how her father's anger about the points of the compass . . . and her own anguish, all had slipped, all had passed, all had streamed away. What then came next? Where were they going?

The answer to her question turns on her memory of her father in his study; she is sitting in the boat with him but remembering an earlier state:

> The old gentlemen in the study she thought could have told her. . . . They were cracking in front of them the pages of *The Times,* when she

came in from the garden, all in a muddle, about something. . . . Just
to please herself she would take a book from the shelf and stand there,
watching her father write. . . . And she thought, standing there with
her book open, one could let whatever one thought expand here like
a leaf in water; and if it did well here, among the old gentlemen smok-
ing . . . then it was right. And watching her father as he wrote in his
study, she thought (now sitting in the boat) he was not vain, nor a
tyrant and did not wish to make you pity him. Indeed, if he saw she was
there, reading a book, he would ask her, as gently as any one could,
Was there nothing he could give her?

Lest this should be wrong, she looked at him reading the little book
with the shiny cover mottled like a plover's egg. No; it was right.

The *Diary* reports a similar context and sentiment, when Virginia
Woolf was about the same age as Cam in the boat:

I think of it with some sentiment—father tramping over the Library
with his little girl sitting at H.P.G. [Hyde Park Gate] in mind. He must
have been 65; I 15 or 16 then; and why I don't know but I became
enraptured, though not exactly interested, but the sight of the large
yellow page entranced me. I used to dream of those obscure adventurers
and no doubt practiced their style in my copybook. (Dec. 8, 1929, p. 150)

Cam shares Virginia Woolf's sentiment for the encounters with her
father in the library, her tendencies to "dream of obscure adventures"
at the same age and her reconciliation of a brilliant daughter's complex
attitudes towards a problematic father. Virginia Woolf, like Cam,
is "telling herself a story but knowing at the same time what was
the truth."

The problem of re-creating and discovering her mother is worked
through twice in the novel, but in different ways. In Part I she is
alive and present, and the author is trying as an artist to shape her
memories of her into a novel. Lily is painting or thinking of painting
Mrs. Ramsay throughout Part I, and not succeeding. In Part III
Lily is painting Mrs. Ramsay from memory (like Virginia Woolf in
Part I) and succeeding, not on canvas, but in her mind, where the
real interactions between memory and art occur. ("One might say,
even of this scrawl, not of that actual picture, perhaps, but of what it
attempted, that it remained for ever.") In some ways then, Lily in
Part III parallels Virginia Woolf writing Part I, and comments on the
nature of writing that part, exchanging "the fluidity of life for the
concentration of painting." Lily reveals in Part III a wide variety of
attitudes towards Mrs. Ramsay that reflect the complexity of a child's
attitude towards a dead parent. She is angry at her "for having gone,
and then having gone, come back again," and she can almost forget
her in spite of her love:

For really, what did she feel, come back after all these years and Mrs. Ramsay dead? Nothing, nothing—nothing that she could express at all.

Mrs. Ramsay dead; Andrew killed; Prue dead too—repeat it as she might, it roused no feeling in her.

. . . she thought she would never feel sorrow for Mrs. Ramsay again. Had she missed her among the coffee cups at breakfast? not in the least.

Part of Lily's problem is the child/artist's problem of introspection. Do I care enough, in the right way?

Remember turning aside at mother's bed, when she had died and Stella took us in, to laugh, secretly, at the nurse crying. She's pretending, I said, aged 13, and was afraid I was not feeling enough. So now. (Sept. 12, 1934, p. 224)

But it is clearly a problem stemming from a deep attachment and admiration, which one can never do full justice to in memory or in art. "Even her shadow at the window . . . was full of authority." That Virginia Woolf came close is reflected in her reports of her sister Vanessa's response to reading the novel: "Nessa enthusiastic—a sublime, almost upsetting spectacle. She says it is an amazing portrait of mother; a supreme portrait painter; has lived in it; found the rising of the dead almost painful." (May 16, 1927, p. 106)

In addition to shaping her attitudes towards her parents, and having "father's character . . . and mother's; and St. Ives; and childhood," the novel reflects some aspects of Virginia Woolf's life that are related to but separable from this dimension. The relationship between Lily and William Bankes is an awkward one even though they care for and respect each other. "Indeed, his friendship had been one of the pleasures of her life. She loved William Bankes." They go for walks together "summer after summer," and Lily helps him buy a carpet for his staircase. He is the only one she tries to talk with about her painting; she is one of the few women he thinks "sensible" and a good companion. But they never marry. The general "feeling" of the relationship is remarkably like that between Virginia Woolf and Lytton Strachey.[11] Strachey proposed to her in 1909, and she accepted, but he withdrew almost immediately. In spite of this they remained friends, saw each other frequently, and respected each other's work at a distance. Although not a "portrait" of the relationship, biographical experience has again contributed something to her treatment of the fictional relationship between Lily and William Bankes.

[11] Cf. *Virginia Woolf and Lytton Strachey: Letters* (London: Hogarth Press, 1956), and Dorothy Brewster, *Virginia Woolf* (New York, N.Y. University Press, 1962), p. 9.

To the Lighthouse is unique among the novels for its focus directly on childhood and parents, and in being located totally in a remote non-urban setting. The two obviously go together, the invisible line between Skye and the city reflecting that between childhood and maturity. But even in Cornwall, the author's concern is still with the kind of people she belonged to and knew well, the intellectual aristocracy of the famous Bloomsbury Group. The Ramsays are *in* but not *of* the inhabitants. Mrs. McNab is a representative of minimal human consciousness, and Macalister and his son, though on the boat, are not present. In her introduction to a book of biographies of working class women, she wrote: "One could not be Mrs. Giles of Durham, because one's body had never stood at the washtub; one's hands had never wrung and scrubbed and chopped up whatever the meat is that makes a miner's supper." [12] Both the novel and this statement reflect the influence of the social dimensions of her life and her method as a novelist. She worked from within, having done or thought what she writes or having a firm ground for exercising intuition. To decry her failure to cover the full social spectrum in her work, as has too often been done, is simply to wish she had been a different person or to lack an awareness of who she was.

For a final but difficult point, it should be noticed that *To the Lighthouse* reflects in its own way what Woolf meant by "all the usual things I try to put in—life, death, etc." Mrs. Ramsay's drive for life, for helping the poor, sending parcels, repairing the greenhouse, covering up the skull with her green shawl, arranging marriages, are based on her intuitive knowledge of her "antagonist," death and decay. At the back of her mind is always the knowledge of this antagonist she is fighting against, and an intuition that in death she might find the rest and calm and permanence in "eternity" which she longs for.

> . . . life being now strong enough to bear her on again, she began all this business, as a sailor not without weariness sees the wind fill his sail and yet hardly wants to be off again and thinks how, had the ship sunk, he would have whirled round and round and found rest on the floor of the sea.

Lily too has such moments in which she feels "her own headlong desire to throw herself off the cliff and be drowned looking for a pearl brooch on a beach." In all her work Virginia Woolf was asserting her life-affirming self against a comparable longing for rest, and the knowledge that it all came to death in the end, which might or might not be a new beginning. In Part II, when the screen door opens to let "Nothing" into the "house without a soul," Virginia

[12] *Life as We Have Known It,* ed. Margaret Davies (London: Leonard and Virginia Woolf, 1931).

Woolf is trying in her imagination to cross the line she stepped over when she walked into the Ouse, the line Septimus crossed when he leaped from the building in *Mrs. Dalloway*. As always, it is a glimpse beneath the waves on the surface, into the unknown depths which she knew she must some day penetrate to complete her life-long search for form:

> So loveliness reigned and stillness, and together made the shape of loveliness itself, a form from which life had parted; solitary like a pool at evening, far distant, seen from a train window, vanishing so quickly that the pool, pale in the evening, is scarcely robbed of its solitude, though once seen. Loveliness and stillness clasped hands in the bedroom, and among the shrouded jugs and sheeted chairs even the prying of the wind, and the soft nose of the clammy sea airs, rubbing, snuffling, and reiterating their questions—"Will you fade? Will you perish?"—scarcely disturbed the peace, the indifference, the air of pure integrity, as if the question they asked scarcely needed that they should answer: we remain.

CHARACTER AND CHARACTERIZATION

> And suddenly the meaning which, for no reason at all, as perhaps they are stepping out of the Tube or ringing a doorbell, descends on people, making them symbolical, making them representative, came upon them. . . .

Once some of the biographical implications of Mr. and Mrs. Ramsay are explored, there is still their existence as characters in a novel, and the problem of the larger significance they gain through Virginia Woolf's treatment of them as fictional characters. "Half one's notions of other people were, after all, grotesque. They served private purposes of one's own," comments Lily in Part III, and the "purposes" of Virginia Woolf as novelist are served by her characters as well as those other purposes I have mentioned.

In trying to define the function of the Ramsays in the novel, several mistakes must be avoided. For Virginia Woolf, the creation of character involved getting at states and qualities of mind, those inner regions from which actions flow. Actions are significant only as they reflect their source, and the opinion one character has of another is often more an index of his own mind than of the character being observed. Even realizing this, it can be difficult to get at the significance of the two Ramsays. James discovers that "nothing was simply one thing," as Lily discovers that "One wanted fifty pairs of eyes to see with. . . . Fifty pairs of eyes were not enough to get round that one woman with . . . her thoughts, her imaginations, her desires."

One of the more common ways to "get round" the Ramsays is to assume that Mr. Ramsay is a negative character, that he is "wrong" in his approach to life, so that the novel is a refutation of his state of mind, and similarly, that Mrs. Ramsay is a positive character and "right," that the novel is a vindication of her point of view. But if we look closely at Mrs. Ramsay, we see that it is *because* she has so dark a sense of life that she must constantly assert her energies against the forces of death and decay.

> There is no reason, order, justice: but suffering, death, the poor. There was no treachery too base for the world to commit; she knew that. No happiness lasted; she knew that.

She knows this, as she knows everything, from within, rather than from looking out at the world. Her short-sightedness is emphasized again and again, reflecting her projective method of knowing by "becoming" intuitively what she perceives. When the voices in the background cease, she looks up "with an impulse of terror," for it is then that she can hear the "sound which had been obscured and concealed under the other sounds," the inner note which her constant business drowned out at other times. She knows that "things get shabbier and shabbier summer after summer," that "things must spoil," yet her reaction is constantly to improve "things," to patch the greenhouse, to make marriages, knowing that they too must spoil. "She felt this thing that she called life terrible, hostile, and quick to pounce on you if you gave it a chance. . . . And yet she had said to all these children, You shall go through it all. To eight people she had said relentlessly that. . . ." Her weapons in the constant struggle with her "antagonist" are people, bits and scraps of things, little parcels tied with string ("one helped oneself out of solitude reluctantly by laying hold of some little odd or end, some sound, some sight"), and her mental faculties are will, "wishing," and "hope." Her struggle is for the most part totally quiet, as she internalizes sights, sounds, and the Lighthouse itself. When James looks at Mr. Ramsay in Part III he realizes that "he had become physically what was always at the back of both of their minds—that loneliness which was for both of them the truth about things." In death, Mrs. Ramsay becomes what was always at the back of her mind.

When she dies, she leaves Mr. Ramsay stumbling along a passage with his arms stretched out, but "his arms, though stretched out, remained empty." The stretching out of the arms is like his looking for the square root of 1253 which has none, like his constant effort "to arrive at a perfectly clear understanding of the problem," his attempt to reason consecutively from *A* to *Z*. In going from *A* to *Z*, he is ironically unable to reach *R*, the letter of his own name. Each time, as he is about to reach *R* as concept, there is a "flash of darkness" in which he can only think of himself, of what others are thinking of him, of whether or not his books will survive. He conceives of *himself* from the outside, for he is *R,* and is therefore constantly making up his character according to external forms. He is self-dramatizing, playing a part, walking up and down, making his life have the only kind of form that he can feel as reality. What he reads must have plot, must survive in time, and his own life must have these qualities too. He must go physically to the Lighthouse, or be going to it; he must have his watch and compass, his boots, for life is to him a process of getting there. Whatever his philosophical theories are, there is no place for them in the book as such; the relation of abstract thought to life, if it has any, is in how it feels to be a person naturally committed to that kind of thought, what life itself is like for that kind of mind.

Mr. Ramsay is always ready to see the difficult side of things, to announce and accept the fact that they cannot go to the Lighthouse "tomorrow," because of a basic confidence that eventually they can go. If he doesn't reach *Z,* someone will, because life is constituted so as to allow it to happen. His inability to look closely at objects, his far-sightedness, is a limitation but a saving one for him. He does not get lost in short-time difficulties, or oppressed by the casualties in "The Charge of The Light Brigade," because he knows that the triumph will be all the greater for the heroic survivors. He lives life as "a perfectly straightforward affair," and life accommodates itself to him, as does the novel, for both allow him his goal of reaching the Lighthouse. In his own way, going to the Lighthouse in III is a reaching out for Mrs. Ramsay, paralleling Lily's activity of painting and reaching back in memory.

If we compare these qualities of mind and life with Mrs. Ramsay, it turns out that his insistence on facing the casualties of life squarely, anticipating them and celebrating them, weeping openly over the death scene in Scott's *The Antiquary,* grows out of a confidence in life which is the opposite of her darkness:

> Why take such a gloomy view of life? he said. It is not sensible. For it was odd; and she believed it to be true; that with all his gloom and desperation he was happier, more hopeful on the whole, than she was.

It is odd, that a mind nourished by violence and disaster should be positive and hopeful; but no more odd than the contradictory tendencies present in Mrs. Ramsay's mind. There is a comfort in conceiving life as "a perfectly straightforward affair," no matter what the nature of that conception.

The Ramsays can be separated in this way, but only to see how they are fused in an active interdependency in the novel—not merely as

husband and wife, but as supplementary components of the life
force and the human imagination. Alone, neither is representative of
life or capable of grasping it completely. She wants a unity and completion, a sense of eternity, that life can give only in moments. He
wants an order and precision (watch, compass, alphabet, etc.) which
can still not find a natural square root for 1253. Mr. Ramsay cannot
account for Mrs. Ramsay, nor she for him; but the novel must account for both fully, for together they represent the fullness of life's
potential. The novel has an ending which is in fact a double ending,
meant to convey "the sense of reading the two things at the same
time." (Sept. 5, 1926, p. 99) One of these "two things" is Mr. Ramsay's
old-fashioned, time-bound, novelistic climax; the other is Lily's "vision." Each of them has repeated, but in different ways, the mental
trip to the Lighthouse taken by Mrs. Ramsay in Part I.

One other character calls for mention here on grounds that he is
universally and undeservedly overlooked in interpretations of the
novel. Augustus Carmichael, the poet, is a constant presence in the
novel, yet he is not presented "from within" as the Ramsays, Lily,
Bankes, James, Cam, Paul, Minta, and even Tansley are:

> But this was one way of knowing people, she thought: to know the
> outline, not the detail. . . .

Lily is speaking of Carmichael, and reflecting the problem of the
reader as well as Mrs. Ramsay. We know that Carmichael is a poet,
that his volume published during the war sold well, that he takes
opium, reads French novels during the day and Vergil at night, and
that he will not let Mrs. Ramsay do little things for him. Mrs. Ramsay
thinks he doesn't like her, and feels uneasy in his presence; yet Carmichael is the only one who speaks her first name in the whole novel
("Ellen, please, another plate of soup."),[13] and he "chants" the words
of Elton's "Luriana Lurilee" at the end of the dinner "as if he did her
homage." Lily feels that he has "crowned the occasion" at the very
end, with his archaic gesture (like Mr. Ramsay sprinkling the crumbs
over the water), and also that he shares with her "some notion . . .
about the ineffectiveness of action, the supremacy of thought."

There is something intriguingly profound about Carmichael that
is crucial to the novel. When she was searching for "a new name for
my books to supplant 'novel,'" the first candidate for the blank space
was "Elegy." Carmichael seems to have mastered the elegiacal as a
way of life, to live life almost from the beyond, "monumental and

---

[13] This detail might not be worth mentioning had several critics not elaborated
the significance of her *not having* a first name. Also, it reflects Virginia Woolf's
penchant for names like Helen, Lily, Eleanor, Susan, Clara, Clarissa, Lucy—all
associated with light, purity and innocence.

contemplative." It may seem odd that it is he who has a second bowl of soup, that his hand reaches for the fruit Mrs. Ramsay was looking at as poetry, but this reflects his reduction of "actual" life to a process of eating, to make room for the supremacy of thought and elegiac contemplation:

> A shadow was on the page; she looked up. It was Augustus Carmichael shuffling past, precisely now, at the very moment when it was painful to be reminded of the inadequacy of human relationships, that the most perfect was flawed, and could not bear the examination . . . it was at this moment when she was fretted thus ignobly in the wake of her exaltation, that Mr. Carmichael shuffled past, in his yellow slippers. . . .

He shuffles past at precisely this point because it is in such moments that the view he represents is needed. Augustus Carmichael punctuates every significant action and section in the book with a reminder that any view large enough to encompass the inadequacy of life and the inevitability of death must depend on the artistic purification of the emotions so that we can look, as Aeneas did, at the "tears in the nature of things."

MEN AND WOMEN

It should be clear enough from a careful reading of the novel that Virginia Woolf's art is essentially androgynous—that she explores both the masculine and the feminine with a profound sense of their interdependence in the economy of mental as well as biological existence. On one level, Mr. Ramsay is more significant as a kind of mind, a point of view, than he is as a male. His masculinity is used to help define that attitude metaphorically, but he is no more a picture of the "male" mind *per se,* than Mrs. Ramsay is of the "female" mind. On this level their sexual relationship reflects the interdependence of two attitudes towards life that are related to but transcend differences in gender.

There is another level in the novel, however, where Virginia Woolf is clearly using the Ramsays to articulate the profound and basic sexual differentiation between the male and female roles in life:

> Mrs. Ramsay, who had been sitting loosely, folding her son in her arm, braced herself, and, half turning, seemed to raise herself with an effort, and at once to pour erect into the air a rain of energy, a column of spray, looking at the same time animated and alive as if all her energies were being fused into force, burning and illuminating (quietly though she sat, taking up her stocking again), and into this delicious fecundity, this fountain and spray of life, the fatal sterility of the male plunged itself, like a beak of brass, barren and bare. . . . It was sympathy he

wanted, to be assured of his genius, first of all, and then to be taken
within the circle of life, warmed and soothed, to have his senses restored
to him, his barrenness made fertile, and all the rooms of the house made
full of life . . . and beyond them the nurseries; they must be furnished,
they must be filled with life.

. . . Standing between her knees, very stiff, James felt all her strength
flaring up to be drunk and quenched by the beak of brass, the arid
scimitar of the male, which smote mercilessly, again and again, demanding sympathy.

Filled with her words, like a child who drops off satisfied, he said, at
last, looking at her with humble gratitude, restored, renewed, that he
would take a turn; he would watch the children playing cricket. He
went.

Although Mrs. Ramsay sits quietly knitting and talking, this scene is
fully and complexly charged with sex, with an emphasis on the
"sterility" of the male and the "fecundity" of the female, seen both
as sexual partner and as mother. Although the emphasis is on the
aggressive, demanding urge of the male, and his sterility, whatever
hostility is present emanates from James who is sitting between Mrs.
Ramsay's knees, acutely aware of his mother's turning all her sexual
energy towards his father. Mrs. Ramsay reflects on a comparable scene
later: "And the whole of the effort of merging and flowing and creating rested on her. Again she felt, as a fact without hostility, the
sterility of men, for if she did not do it nobody would. . . ." We must
contemplate this scene, and the view of sexual difference it gives,
as a "fact without hostility," for the other side is represented too:

. . . she let it uphold her and sustain her, this admirable fabric of the
masculine intelligence, which ran up and down, crossed this way and
that, like iron girders spanning the swaying fabric, upholding the world,
so that she could trust herself to it utterly, even shut her eyes, or
flicker them for a moment. . . .

Lily cannot begin to finish her paintings in Part III until she has acknowledged Mr. Ramsay's masculinity and his needs, and discovered
that even in an absurd comment on his boots she could present herself
as a woman, and receive something in doing so as well as give something. She had contemplated earlier, at the dinner, a more mundane
application of the reciprocity of this relationship:

There is a code of behaviour, she knew, whose seventh article . . . says
that on occasions of this sort it behooves the woman . . . to go to the
help of the young man opposite . . . as indeed it is their duty, she
reflected, in her old maidenly fairness, to help us, suppose the Tube were

to burst into flames. Then, she thought, I should certainly expect Mr. Tansley to get me out. But how would it be, she thought, if neither of us did either of these things?

On this level the social fabric rests on reciprocal sexuality as, on other levels, artistic creation and the continuation of life depend on it.

Even James, whose hostility causes him to carry into adolescence "this old symbol of taking a knife and striking his father to the heart" is able at last to see that "it was not him, that old man reading, whom he wanted to kill, but it was the thing that descended on him—without his knowing it perhaps." There is some impersonal driving force acting through the male which can be recognized but not accounted for:

> Suppose then that as a child sitting helpless in a perambulator, or on someone's knee, he had seen a waggon crush ignorantly and innocently, some one's foot? . . . But the wheel was innocent. So now, when his father came striding down the passage knocking them up early in the morning to go to the Lighthouse down it came over his foot, over Cam's foot, over anybody's foot. One sat and watched it.

James, as he steers the boat, tacking upwind towards the Lighthouse, watching his father, shares this force with him and finally recognizes it in himself. "He looked at his father reading fiercely with his legs curled tight. They shared that knowledge. 'We are driving before a gale—we must sink,' he began saying to himself, half aloud, exactly as his father said it." Mr. Ramsay's triumphant "Well done!" seems more to acknowledge this rite of passage in his son than the mere steering of the boat to the island.

There may be an inherent defensiveness in the male point of view that is unable to take Virginia Woolf's presentation of the "fatal sterility of the male" as a "fact without hostility." There is also an opportunity, sometimes exercised, for female readers to take the novel as a feminist tract, asserting the superiority of the female over the male. The novel will not support such a view. What it will support, and demands, is a reading that goes beyond the biological and sees her view of sex as one aspect of the dialectical economy of human existence:

> Thus one portion of being is the Prolific, the other the devouring: to the Devourer it seems as if the producer was in his chains; but it is not so, he only takes portions of existence and fancies that the whole.

> But the Prolific would cease to be Prolific unless the Devourer, as a sea, received the excess of his delights. (Blake, "The Marriage of Heaven and Hell")

BOOKS

The grandmother retired to her nook, the mother mechanically took in her hand her tattered Bible, and seemed to read, though her eyes were drowned with tears. (Scott's *The Antiquary*)

. . . so she turned and felt on the table beside her for a book. (Mrs. Ramsay, Part I)

If I have to wait, I read; if I wake in the night, I feel along the shelf for a book. (Bernard in *The Waves*)

Well, if Cam would not answer him, he would not bother her Mr. Ramsay decided, feeling in his pocket for a book. (Part III)

One of the most important features of the novel, one which is too often ignored, is its "bookishness." All the characters are readers, and the act of reading, including what is read, is a reflection of and clue to character in all cases. At first glance the act of reading would seem to be a gesture of retirement, a turning away from society and from life. When the "great clangour of the gong" sounds the call for dinner in Part I, everyone is summoned from scattered places "in attics, in bedrooms, on little perches of their own, reading, writing . . . to leave all that . . . and the novels on the bed-tables, and the diaries which were so private. . . ." During the dinner, when the conversation turns on the Waverley Novels and ends in a poetry recitation, Lily, Tansley, and Bankes are constantly longing for a return to their private worlds of work and art and books; it is this force that Mrs. Ramsay must overcome if she is to knit the group together in more than the conventional social order represented by Lily's image of the chairman requesting everyone to speak in French for the sake of "some order, some uniformity." Yet the triumphant ending of the dinner turns on bringing "books" into the group, both in discussing the fate of the Waverly Novels and, finally, in reciting aloud Charles Elton's "Luriana Lurilee" as an implicit tribute to Mrs. Ramsay. The irony of Elton's being a poet not read (he isn't represented in any of the many editions of *The Oxford Book of English Verse*) is no doubt deliberate. Even *his* poem can be read, and more than read—as it is "chanted" it joins and climaxes the harmony of the group in a deliberate echo of a religious service. The involvement in living calls us away from books and art, but the movement is circular, for art can then reflect and structure the moods and rhythms of non-bookish life, can perhaps give it or at least suggest a different form of that "eternity" which Mrs. Ramsay can find only glimpses of.

Mrs. McNab, Mrs. Bast, stayed the corruption and the rot; rescued from the pool of Time that was fast closing over them now a basin, now a cupboard; fetched up from oblivion all the Waverley novels and a tea set. . . .

Within this general use of books, there is a more specific function that deserves comment and reflection. The kind of books one reads, and even the manner in which one reads them, are reflections of character and the different ways in which reality is available to the different characters in the novel. The melodramatic Mr. Ramsay reads Scott, and recites Tennyson's "Charge of the Light Brigade" and Cowper's "The Castaway." The intuitive Mrs. Ramsay reads a fairy tale to her children and a Shakespeare sonnet to herself. The inscrutable Carmichael reads Vergil at night and French novels during the day; the "judicial" Bankes reads Carlyle and wonders if Carlyle's life was not a refutation of his books, and if the books will survive by being brought to life in the existence of a new Carlylean hero.

Even more important than what they read is how they read it. Mr. Ramsay reads and recites for the play-acting which is his life; his own living merges with and is shaped by what he reads, and therefore his concern for Scott's survival is a concern for his own ("—if young men did not care for this, naturally they did not care for him either."). His act of reading Scott is a self-serving, self-defining act on several levels. As he reads the sections of *The Antiquary* on Mucklebackit's cottage and Steenie's drowning and funeral, he revives Scott, gains emotional comfort ("the astonishing delight and feeling of vigour that it gave him") as well as material for future lectures and books of his own. His generalized vindication of Scott is made personal and particular later, when he must share with Mucklebackit the loss of his own son. In most of Part III he sits "reading fiercely" to the end of his book, the end of his trip to the Lighthouse, and his part of the end of the novel. We don't know what the mysterious little book is, but we do know that its shiny cover is "mottled like a plover's egg," and that it has written on the flyleaf "that he had spent fifteen francs on dinner; the wine had been so much; he had given so much to the waiter; all was added up neatly at the bottom of the page. But what might be written in the book which had rounded its edges off in his pocket, she did not know." Cam's not knowing the contents of the book parallels her not being able to penetrate the innerness of Mr. Ramsay himself. For him, the egg-like book reflects the mystery of life and his attitude towards it—his fierce reading is his attempt to find it all "added up neatly at the bottom of the page." Whether or not his book in Part III is *The Antiquary* which he was reading in Part I, his reading of it, and the conclusive "Well done" which comments on the book as well as James' handling of the boat, go beyond and end the "suspense" he was left in at the earlier phase:

> But he must read it again. He could not remember the whole shape of the thing. He had to keep his judgment in suspense.

In his own time-bound way (from *A* to *Z*) he has at the end found "the whole shape of the thing," as Lily has found her whole shape in the act of painting.

Mrs. Ramsay's reading too is intertwined with her life and reflects her approach to it. As her life is consumed in the living, so is the Army and Navy Stores catalogue cut into bits and pieces and used up, each bit "endowed . . . with heavenly bliss." The story of "The Fisherman and His Wife" has an intuitive relationship to her own situation which she can sense rhythmically but not conceptually. As she reads the sonnet, not following the words but internalizing its rhythm and formal compactness, she has her equivalent of the "delight and feeling of vigour" that Mr. Ramsay gets from reading Scott:

> . . . and so reading she was ascending, she felt, on to the top, on to the summit. How satisfying! How restful! All the odds and ends of the day stuck to this magnet; her mind felt swept, felt clean. And then there it was, suddenly entire; she held it in her hands, beautiful and reasonable, clear and complete, the essence sucked out of life and held rounded here—the sonnet.

As the two read together in their different ways, they reflect Mr. Ramsay's notion of the two classes of men: ". . . on the one hand the steady goers of superhuman strength who, plodding and persevering, repeat the whole alphabet in order . . . on the other the gifted, the inspired who, miraculously, lump all the letters together in one flash—the way of genius." And as Mr. Ramsay's choice of Mucklebackit's cottage is confirmed by the later shape of things, Mrs. Ramsay's choice prefigures her own absence and Lily's attempt to find and create the "whole shape of the thing" on the "uncompromising white stare" of her canvas:

> Nor did I wonder at the lily's white,
> Nor praise the deep vermillion in the rose;
> They were but sweet, but figures of delight,
> Drawn after you, you pattern of all those.
> Yet seem'd it winter still, and, you away,
> As with your shadow I with these did play.

In even the minor characters the attitudes towards books and life are fused. Tansley carries with him always a "purple book," proudly announcing to the world that he has reduced his life and life itself to the world of books. Paul Rayley, who is well-meaning but can never quite make things last or work his way, is an ironic example of the way books can reflect life. "They lasted, he said. He had read some of Tolstoi at school. There was one he always remembered, but he had forgotten the name. . . . 'Vronsky,' said Paul. He remembered that because he always thought it such a good name for a villain." Our last view of Paul finds him in a situation of "tolerated" adultery like that in *Anna Karenina*. Minta, who is always careless, losing her brooch, borrowing and losing books, "had left the third volume of *Middlemarch* in the train and she never knew what had happened in the end; but afterwards she got on perfectly. . . ." In spite of the similarities between the Rayleys and the Lydgates (in *Middlemarch*), things do seem to work out for them in a way that would have been impossible in the worlds of Tolstoi and George Eliot. "They're happy like that. . . . Life has changed completely," muses Lily, and Paul and Minta reflect the change in their own way as Lily does in hers. Mr. Carmichael's book, brought out in the spring during the war, sells well, for that is when people are receptive to the shadowy reminder of mortality his presence brings to the novel. Even Mrs. McNab's song ("something that had been gay twenty years before on the stage . . . was robbed of meaning, was like the voice of witlessness, humour, persistency itself, trodden down but springing up again") reflects her minimal but persistent consciousness and parallels the focus of the novel in Part II.

On a larger scale, two "books" have a relationship to the novel very much like that which Mrs. Ramsay recognizes in "The Fisherman and His Wife."

> . . . for the story of the Fisherman and his Wife was like the bass gently accompanying a tune, which now and then ran up unexpectedly into the melody.

The fairy tale is about a "Fisherman who lived with his wife in a pig-stye close by the sea, and everyday he went out fishing; and he fished, and he fished." There are numerous parallels or "resonances" (Virginia Woolf's word) between the tale and the novel. The flounder the fisherman catches is released to return to the bottom, "leaving a long streak of blood behind him," as the fish is returned to the sea in Part III. Mrs. Ramsay's comment comes at a moment when she has just read the Fisherman's refrain (". . . For my wife, good Ilsabil,/ Wills not as I'd have her will."), and the clash of wills runs "into the melody" in Part I again and again over the issue of the trip to the Lighthouse. But even more important is the way the tale reflects the larger rhythms and meanings of *To the Lighthouse*. In her earliest mention of the novel, Woolf said only that "the sea is to be heard all through it." (June 27, 1925, p. 80) In the tale, the sea is progressively turbulent and chaotic each time the Fisherman goes out to obtain a newer and more presumptuous wish from the Flounder. On his last trip the Fisherman must go into a storm which rivals the "gigantic chaos" of Part II, Section VII, to ask for the impossible wish, "to be like unto God," to control the cosmic elements and forces themselves. This demand reflects Mrs. Ramsay's desire for more than life can offer. In some ways—in the eyes of her admirers—she is already a King, an Emperor and a Pope, but her basic demands are more than material ones. She would like things not so shabby, and fifty pounds to repair the greenhouse roof, but her real wish is to make the rainbow permanent rather than "ephemeral" as she recognizes it to be in Part I; and the only means she has, like the Fisherman's wife, are wishes.

If we look at Scott's *The Antiquary*, which Mr. Ramsay reads in Part I and may be reading in Part II, we find that it too runs up into the melody and has a contrapuntal relationship with "The Fisherman and His Wife." The setting for *The Antiquary* is among the fishing villages on the friths of Forth and Tay in Scotland. In part, the action takes place in and around the cottage of the fisherman Mucklebackit, which is Scott's equivalent of the "pig-stye close by the sea" in the tale and the Ramsays' house in the novel:

> I wish I could say that its inside was well arranged, decently furnished, or tolerably clean. On the contrary, I am compelled to admit, there was confusion,—there was delapidation,—there was dirt good store.[14]

There are similarities between Mucklebackit and his son and Macalister and his boy, and many particular parallels that might be pointed out, but I shall mention only a few important ones. In the same chapter Steenie, the most promising Mucklebackit son, is out on an expedition as Andrew is in Part I, and the possibility of danger to him and of burning the dinner occur to his mother as they do to Mrs. Ramsay:

> I wonder what that auld daft beggar carle and our son Steenie can be doing out in sic a night as this. . . . Gang awa, ane o' ye, hinnies, up to the heugh head, and gie them a cry in case they're within hearing; the car-cakes will be burnt to a cinder.

The aura of specialness around Steenie is like that around Andrew, and both are marked by the fates for premature death—Steenie by drowning (Chap. 29) and Andrew in the War.

The character in Scott most like Mrs. Ramsay is the grandmother, Luckie Elspeth (cf. Ilsabil, Ellen), the "gudemither," the "old sibyl," who has alternating moods of naive cheerfulness and dark despair,

[14] Vol. II, Ch. xxvi.

as well as intermittent periods of "uncanny" lucidity and vision. "—But see as our gudemither's hands and lips are ganging—now it's working in her head like barm—she'll speak eneugh the night. Whiles she'll no speak a word in a week, unless it be to the bits o' bairns." The Antiquary (Oldbuck) is in many ways similar to Carmichael. He lives in a different world and time from the actions he observes and comments on, and can see popular customs only as they relate to the ancient models which constitute his test of reality. As Carmichael stands, "surveying, tolerantly and compassionately, their final destiny," Lily senses that he has "crowned the occasion . . . when his hand slowly fell, as if she had seen him let fall from his great height a wreath of violets and asphodels which, fluttering slowly, lay at length upon the earth"—a gesture which seems to include the whole essence of the pastoral elegy. The Antiquary's final gesture strikes the same note as Carmichael's:

> . . . Lord Geraldin was married to Miss Wardour, the Antiquary making the lady a present of the wedding ring—a massy circle of antique chasing, bearing the motto of Aldobrand Oldenbuck, *Kunst macht gunst.*

The motto ("Art makes things come out all right") fits Scott's novel on the level of artifice, as the plot is conventionally tied up, the mysteries accounted for and the miscellaneous characters tucked safely into permanent niches. But it fits Woolf's novel in a much more complex sense, as art becomes the realm of fulfillment for its character's aspirations, and the only way to bring form into an otherwise chaotic existence.

The question inevitably arises, does one *have* to read "The Fisherman and His Wife," *The Antiquary,* Carlyle, *Anna Karenina, Middlemarch,* Shakespeare, Vergil, Tennyson, Cowper, Elton and the others in order to understand the novel. It is here that the connections I have been pointing out between the novels and other works elude the conventional modes of interpretation. To make them conscious, to "explicate" them, is to risk missing the way in which for Virginia Woolf the experience of literary allusion is an integral part of the experience of life. The way one "experiences" an allusion in her work is different from the conscious recognition that *x* in Scott is like *y* in Woolf; it is more like the vague but urgent sense of importance and resonance that the characters in the novel get from their own reading. One's sense of structure or form in one's own life comes from models available in books, but also from popular songs, films, cultural myths, inspirational works—the whole realm of available patterns of experience, ranging from the conscious to the peripherally conscious. Mrs. Ramsay's image of the accompanying bases running now and then up into the melody suggests the intuitive and experiential quality of allusion or association. It is like sensing the relationship between two tunes without being able to analyze it in technical terms, or sensing in a later movement an echo or development of an earlier passage in the same score. The musical analogy is inevitable for this kind of relationship, as it is for Mrs. Ramsay's sense of relationship between herself and Mr. Ramsay in "that solace which two different notes, one high, one low, struck together, seem to give each other as they combine." It is a "resonance" which dies even as it is being felt, and it is a part of the music of the novel:

> And now . . . there rose that half-heard melody, that intermittent music which the ear half catches but lets fall . . . loud, low, but mysteriously related; which the ear strains to bring together and is always on the verge of harmonizing, but they are never quite heard, never fully harmonized, and at last, in the evening, one after another the sounds die out, and the harmony falters, and silence falls.

STRUCTURE AND FORM

> How tired I am of stories; how tired I am of phrases that come down beautifully with all their feet on the ground. Also, how I distrust neat designs of life upon half sheets of notepaper. . . . I begin to seek some design in accordance with those moments of humiliation and triumph that come now and then undeniably . . . then is the confusion, the height, and movement. . . . Of story, of design I do not see a trace then. (Bernard in *The Waves*)

For Virginia Woolf the world exists primarily as it can be shaped in the human mind; the "can" here suggests the limits and particularities of the various individual minds, but also the complexities, obstinacies and opacities of whatever component of experience comes from outside the mind. For her the novel must reflect both sides of the problem; she must discover and express the innerness of her characters as they make themselves and their worlds, but she is responsible also for the final context, the external dimension of their experience. One obvious way to achieve the desired innerness is to have the novel enter the consciousness of the characters. But her basic technique here is not limited to the usual notion of a stream-of-consciousness. Her own phrase "decorated processes of thought" is much more precise and suggestive. In this technique the physical world around a character takes on the form of the thought, reflects it and comments on it in a very deliberate and highly developed manner:

> He slipped, seeing before him that hedge which had over and over again rounded some pause, signified some conclusion, seeing his wife and child, seeing again the urns with the trailing red geraniums which had so

often decorated processes of thought, and bore, written up among their leaves, as if they were scraps of paper on which one scribbles notes in the rush of reading—he slipped. . . .

The characters in the novel "decorate" their own thoughts in a variety of ways. They do it in the quick, intuitive way Mr. Ramsay does, or in the more conscious and artistic manner of Lily. "It was odd, she thought, how if one was alone, one leant to inanimate things; trees, streams, flowers; felt they expressed one; felt they became one. . . ." Or it can be even less conscious and more arbitrary, as when Lily "quite unconsciously and incongruously, used the branches of the elm trees outside to help her to stabilize her position." Some of the links are more deliberately artistic and suggestive, as when in Part III the calm and the "great scroll of smoke" reflect Lily's discovery of "one of those globed compacted things over which thought lingers, and love plays," and echo its loss as well:

> But the wind had freshened, and, as the sky changed slightly and the sea changed slightly and the boats altered their positions, the view, which a moment before had seemed miraculously fixed, was now unsatisfactory.

Lily does not know the extent of the connection here, any more than Minta knows the full connection between the loss of her brooch and the loss of innocence it suggests for all the young people out on the walk.

> . . . it might be true that she minded losing her brooch, but she wasn't crying only for that. She was crying for something else. We might all sit down and cry, she felt, but she didn't know what for.

In these cases, and the many others like them, there is a need both for the characters and for the author to link up the processes of thought or intuition with the outside world. As James was struggling with his memories of the past and his present attitude towards his father, "he sought an image to cool and detach and round off his feeling in a concrete shape." He does find such an image in his notion of the "innocent wheel" crushing the foot, as he finds a double image of the Lighthouse (both misty and stark) to reflect his problem of discovering the reality of things.

One of the persistent features of these images is that they do not last; they give way in the minds of the characters to a flux where there is no possibility of a clarifying image, of a formal link with the world outside of mind. There is a danger in recognizing the way in which Virginia Woolf creates world and mind as echoes of each other, and then relegating the whole novel to an assertion of this phase of experience as the final one. Bernard says "of story, of design I do not see a trace *then*," but because he does not see it then does not mean that it isn't there, ready to reassert itself when he is ready to feel it and perceive it. The larger shape of the novel for Virginia Woolf must include "moments of humiliation and triumph" because the basic nature of human consciousness for her is momentary. But when such moments are the basic units of experience, the artist's difficulty, like that of her characters, is in relating these moments, finding an order or pattern or form "among" them. Mrs. Ramsay is able to feel that "We are in the hands of the Lord," and almost at the same moment to wonder "How could the Lord have made this world?" What sustains her are those intermittent moments of intuitive form which descend like Grace, assuring her that "It is enough." Her approach to vision is to tinker with her bits and pieces of available experience while she waits for such moments to come.

For her it is enough, but for the artist something more is needed. Lily senses that "beneath the colour there was the shape," and her sense of that "shape" is of something tangible yet inaccessible:

> She saw the colour burning on a framework of steel; the light of a butterfly's wing lying upon the arches of a cathedral. Of all that only a few random marks scrawled upon the canvas remained.

Her problem is the painter's equivalent to the problem of the novelist who sees consciousness as a constant flux, unstructured, with the past living in the present along with the future which can only take the shape the mind is prepared to give it. If her surface is the activity of characters making themselves and their worlds, how can she suggest or discover the framework of steel which holds them all together? Virginia Woolf's solution is deliberately to choose a form which is purely arbitrary and abstract, like that of painting—calling attention to itself, not pretending to be "natural" or "realistic." Although the execution is complex, the rationale is simple: if experience does not present an observable pattern, if its form in time seems arbitrary and unpredictable, then the artist is free to create an arbitrary form as a context for the experience she seeks to express.

As Mrs. Ramsay sits in the chair in the drawing-room window she presents "to Lily's eyes, an august shape; the shape of a dome." Yet this rounded dome of life comes out in Lily's painting as a "triangular purple shape," not recognizable as "human."

> Mother and child then—objects of universal veneration, and in this case the mother was famous for her beauty—might be reduced . . . to a purple shadow without irreverence.

Lily objects that her picture "was not of them," but a "tribute" which "took that form." The tribute is like the shadow cast by Mrs. Ramsay ("As with your shadow I with these did play") but it is not simply a picture of a shadow. The notion of shadow governs the relationship between the pictorial image and what it is a tribute to:

> Mercifully, whoever it was stayed still inside; had settled by some stroke of luck so as to throw an odd-shaped triangular shadow over the step. It altered the composition of the picture a little. It was interesting. It might be useful.

In a way which Lily cannot directly know, her painting echoes Mrs. Ramsay's sense of "being oneself, a wedge-shaped core of darkness, something invisible to others." The goal is to achieve a sense of felt form in which the means—the particular formal elements—are arbitrary because the inner essence captured by the form is invisible:

> But solitude will be good for a new book. Of course, I shall make friends. I shall be external outwardly. I shall buy some good clothes and go out into new houses. All the time I shall attack *this angular shape in my mind*. I think *The Moths* (if that is what I shall call it) will be *very sharply cornered.* . . . In old days books were so many sentences *absolutely struck with an axe out of crystal:* and now my mind is so impatient, so quick, in some ways so desperate. (March 28, 1929, p. 142 [italics mine])

The artist is free from conventional chronology, free from the presentations of "actions" in any naturalistic way, but not free from the artistic demands of form. Some of the angular elements in the structure of *To the Lighthouse* are often overlooked even though they deliberately call attention to themselves as arbitrary and formal. The real time of the novel occupies parts of two days set ten years apart. The first day moves from about 6:00 in the evening until precisely 12:00 midnight when Mr. Carmichael puts down his Vergil and blows out his candle. The second day moves from sometime before 8:00 in the morning until noon of the same day. The formal division of the book, however, does not conform to these periods of time; the first period spills over into Part II and the second starts towards the end of Part II.

A first reading of Part I tends to be overwhelmed by the simultaneity of much of its action. Mrs. Ramsay's knitting or reading is going on through much of it; Lily is painting until Section IV, then putting up her brushes until the very end of Section IX. Mr. Ramsay is storming around, reciting poetry and scowling. The different characters intersect each other suddenly, and give rise to numerous multiple visions of each other, including memories of the past fused with present perceptions and meditations. This phase of Part I stops suddenly and definitively "when the great clangour of the gong announced solemnly, authoritatively, that all those scattered about . . . must leave all that . . . and assemble in the dining room for dinner."

The possibility of a pun in "authoritatively" is confirmed by the next phase of Part I. Although sitting together at dinner, the characters continue their multiple private existences, conforming reluctantly only to the limited conventional proprieties of social role-playing. They are juxtaposed but not united. This phase of interaction is explored until it almost breaks down, as Mr. Ramsay ("He hated everything dragging on for hours like this.") cannot accept Carmichael's request for another bowl of soup:

> Everybody could see, Mrs. Ramsay thought. There was Rose gazing at her father, there was Roger gazing at his father; both would be off in spasms of laughter in another second, she knew, and so she said promptly (indeed it was time):
> "Light the candles," and they jumped up instantly and went and fumbled at the sideboard.

The lighting of the candles announces and accompanies a new phase in which "they were all conscious of making a party together in a hollow, on an island; had their common cause against that fluidity out there." The expedition returns from the beach precisely at the moment of unveiling the *Boeuf en Daube,* itself a "triumph" with which to "celebrate the occasion." As the dinner ends the voices mingle as if they were "at a service in a cathedral," reminding Mrs. Ramsay of "the Latin words of a service in some Roman Catholic cathedral." Mrs. Ramsay then punctuates the end of this phase as she had the beginning:

> It was necessary now to carry everything a step further. With her foot on the threshold she waited a moment longer in a scene which was vanishing even as she looked, and then, as she moved and . . . left the room, it changed, it shaped itself differently; it had become . . . already the past.

The end of Part I moves back and forth between the minds of Mr. and Mrs. Ramsay (as Part III moves between Lily and the boat) until they are united in their moment of unspoken intimacy.

Part II begins with the gradual ending of the day, as the lights go out, the characters go to sleep, and the author's voice begins to take over. By the time Mr. Carmichael puts out his candle, it is midnight and he is in brackets. The use of brackets throughout Part II is a formal sign of the turning inside-out of the focus of the novel which Part II achieves. In Part I the minds of the characters had been central; whatever was behind or under them, the darkness within Mrs. Ramsay or outside the window, the hands of the author (like Mrs. Ramsay's "hands of the Lord") were only glimpsed. Now the other dimension of the novel steps forward; human concerns and life are brief and trivial, almost instantaneous, and relegated to the background. In Part II we enter the novel's counterpart to the sleep of the characters and the rhythm of the day's cycle. We enter sleep, death, chaos, nothingness, a house without a soul, a world without a consciousness except that of the author, now symbolized by the flashing light which shines into the empty house:

> When darkness fell, the stroke of the Lighthouse, which had laid itself *with such authority* upon the carpet in the darkness, *tracing its pattern,* came now in the softer light of spring mixed with moonlight gliding gently as if it laid its caress and lingered stealthily and looked and came lovingly again. (italics mine)

In Part I Mrs. Ramsay had put her green shawl over the picture frame and over the skull; in Part II it must give way, both to the "frame" of the author's deliberate control and to the death's skull which is the author's "antagonist" as well as Mrs. Ramsay's. In the *Diary* Virginia Woolf referred to Part II as "this impersonal thing, which I am dared to do by my friends, the flight of time and the consequent break of unity in my design. . . ." (July 20, 1925, p. 80)

> Yesterday I finished the first part of *To the Lighthouse,* and today began the second. I cannot make it out—here is the most difficult abstract piece of writing—I have to give an empty house, no people's characters, the passage of time, all eyeless and featureless with nothing to cling to.
> . . . (April 30, 1926, p. 88)

The difficulty is pointed out in the novel too: ". . . no image with semblance of serving and divine promptitude comes readily to hand bringing the night to order and making the world reflect the compass of the soul. The hand dwindles in his hand; the voice bellows in his ear."

As a consequence, nothing could be more arbitrary and less lifelike than the symbolic and even punning descent into nothingness ("sharing a joke with nothingness"; "the kitchen door . . . swung wide; admitted nothing; and slammed to"; "her eyes fell on nothing directly"; the house "without a soul in it"). The novel can even isolate the precise moment when the house almost ceases to exist:

> For now had come that moment, that hesitation when dawn trembles and night pauses, when if a feather alight in the scale it will be weighed down. One feather, and the house, sinking, falling, would have turned and pitched downwards to the depths of darkness.

It is no accident that the moment when the house almost loses its recognizable shape as a house coincides with the moment when the novel is most deliberately and obviously revealed as being shaped by the author. Mrs. McNab had left the house two pages before, with her confused memories of the cook:

And the cook's name now? Mildred? Marian?—some name like that. Ah, she had forgotten—she did forget things. Fiery, like all red-haired women. Many a laugh they had had. She was always welcome in the kitchen. She made them laugh, she did. Things were better then than now.

She re-enters two pages later to begin staying the corruption and the rot, to save the house and the Waverley Novels and *To the Lighthouse* as well, with the same reverie:

> There was the cook now, Mildred, Marian, some such name as that—a red-headed woman, quick-tempered like all her sort, but kind, too. . . . Many a laugh they had had together. . . . They lived well in those days.

As she wrote Part II, Virginia Woolf seemed aware of its special nature which both allowed and demanded that her freedom be brought out into the open:

> . . . well, I rush at it, and at once scatter out two pages. Is it nonsense, is it brilliance? Why am I so flown with words and apparently free to do exactly what I like? When I read a bit it seems spirited too; needs compressing, but not much else. (April 30, 1926, p. 89)

She was aware of the danger of too much of this kind of writing: "But that becomes arty, Liberty greenery yallery somehow: symbolic in loose robes" (May 28, 1929, p. 143). But she also knew, with Lily, that "A light here required a shadow there," and that "It was a question . . . how to connect this mass on the right hand with that on the left. . . . But the danger was that by doing that the unity of the whole might be broken." If the unity of the whole is a rhythm rather than a static structure, then it seems essential for the rhythm of narration, with alternating "presence" and "absence" of the author, to reflect that on-going rhythm rather than to adopt an absolutely fixed form.

As the deliberately exaggerated "presence" of the author recedes towards the end of Part II, naturalistic detail is allowed back in for signalling structural movement. At the very end Mr. Carmichael shuts his book and falls asleep just as he did at the beginning, and the morning after "the sun lifted the curtains, broke the veil on their eyes, and Lily Briscoe stirring in her sleep. . . . Here she was again, she thought, sitting bolt upright in bed. Awake." This phase of Part III centers on the encounter with Mr. Ramsay before his departure for the Lighthouse; it ends simultaneously with the beginning of the final phase:

> And then, she recalled, there was that sudden revivification, that sudden flare . . . which too passed and changed . . . into that other final phase which was new to her and had, she owned, made herself ashamed of her

own irritability, when it seemed as if he had shed worries and ambitions . . . had entered some other region. . . . An extraordinary face! The gate banged.

The banging of the gate is like the clanging of the dinner gong in Part I. It signals a new and final phase of the novel. This final phase has its own complex internal structure, for the novel, like Lily, is "curiously divided, as if one part of her were drawn out there—." There is a constant formal shift back and forth between Lily and the boat, a movement which is intended to reflect the "links" which are being formed in the invisible realms of consciousness, between the past and the present, between Lily and Mrs. Ramsay, Lily and Mr. Ramsay, James and his father, and Cam and her father—and between all of them and the symbolic potential of the Lighthouse. The intermittent moods of calm and breeze, and the tacking of the boat are carefully timed to express the structure and rhythm of the novel; the image of Mr. Ramsay as conductor suggests both the musical nature of the rhythm and the firm control of the author:

> He only raised his right hand mysteriously high in the air, and let it fall upon his knee again as if he were conducting some secret symphony.

As in a symphony, the different parts are resolved in a final chord, in which Mr. Ramsay leaps onto the rock, Mr. Carmichael makes his gesture which crowns the occasion, and Lily adds the final line as she sees the blurred canvas "clear for a second."

THE END

> But for a moment I had sat on the turf somewhere high above the flow of the sea and the sounds of the weeds, had seen the house, the garden, and the waves breaking. The old nurse who turns the pages of the picture-book had stopped and had said, "Look. This is the truth."
> (Bernard in *The Waves*)

> "And that's the end," she said, and she saw in his eyes, as the interest of the story died away in them, something else take its place. . . .

For Virginia Woolf, as for Lily Briscoe, art is the discovery of form through the process of "making," and all the characters in the novel are artists of their own experience. But within this general fusion of art and life, there is a significant distinction between Mrs. Ramsay as an artist in and of "life," and Lily as an artist of a different order. Mrs. Ramsay's vision is centered in the day-to-day struggle to achieve moments of felt relationship and intimations of the future. For her the past is still frozen, still there, available to re-experience in the original form. On the positive side, hers is a world of "reality"—she knits real sox, has real children, and her "tender piece of eternity" is a succulent bite of beef. But there are limits inherent in her medium. Life, like the stocking for Sorley's little boy, is "too short . . . ever so much too short," and nothing can last. The catalogue is consumed in use, the green shawl goes, the Rayleys' marriage is not what she had hoped, her fears rather than her hopes are realized in Prue and Andrew, the beef is eaten, the dinner ends, and the house itself is brought to the brink of annihilation. She has, in Robert Lowell's phrase, "man's lovely,/ peculiar power to choose life and die—," for her own life reflects the self-consuming nature of her art:

> With her foot on the threshold she waited a moment longer in a scene which was vanishing even as she looked, and then, as she moved and . . . left the room, it changed, it shaped itself differently; it had become, she knew, giving one last look at it over her shoulder, already the past.

In an obvious sense Lily's art is a lesser thing than Mrs. Ramsay's art of life. It deals with angles rather than domes, and plays with shadows rather than lives. It is a mode of creating form which is handicapped by the presence of its object but helped by distance and time. As she paints in Part III her art can be seen as a special mode of memory; her materials are not life "now" but are life-as-memory, life as past re-created in the present. But some involvement with life in the present is crucial. When she was using her canvas as a barrier between her and Mr. Ramsay, "She had taken the wrong brush . . . and her easel, rammed into the earth so nervously, was at the wrong angle." She must commit herself to life before she can exchange "the fluidity of life for the concentration of painting," and she must keep stepping away from the canvas to look for the boat, in order to keep in contact with the fluidity of life and avoid being trapped again in a sterile form. For her, then, art is a form of active memorializing, a special way of seeing the past and continuing its relevance in the present. It is active, for "the vision must be perpetually remade." It is memorializing, for "one had constantly a sense of repetition—of one thing falling where another had fallen, and so setting up an echo which chimed in the air and made it full of vibrations."

In spite of the relative strengths and weaknesses of their different modes of vision, art for both Lily and Mrs. Ramsay is a clarification of life achieved within life itself. As such Lily's art shares with Mrs. Ramsay's the basic limitations of life; its eternity is not in the canvas to be "hung in the attics" any more than Mrs. Ramsay's is in the beef to be eaten and digested. This point needs to be emphasized, for the temptation at the end is to take Lily's vision for something of a far different order from what it is, as a "thing" rather than a state of mind.

Like most modern novelists, Virginia Woolf sought constantly for an end that both was and was not an "end" in the conventional sense. To have gotten somewhere, to have said something, revealed something, captured a life or an event in its finished entirety, is both the goal and the one thing the novel indicates cannot be done. Nothing in experience, or in the novel itself, has this quality, so how can the conclusion have it? Yet the end gives us signals of completion. The Lighthouse is reached, Lily adds her line, has her vision; it is almost impossible to resist finding here what we want to find, and what the characters want to find: Mr. Ramsay has become humanized; Lily has discovered an eternal visionary truth; the ghost of Mrs. Ramsay is laid to rest. But the "line" which Lily adds is not the line on the canvas. It is the intuitive, internal "vision" of the rhythm and inter-connectedness of experience; it is also the hard, firm line missing before in the shades, masses and pastels of Paunceforte's coloration. It is the internal linkage between Mrs. Ramsay alive in Part I and dead in Part II, invisible, a thing of memory and memorializing or elegiac art. But it also reflects and partakes of the Ramsayan, old-fashioned sense of plot as completion in time, a literal going to the Lighthouse in broad daylight and at high noon. All of these aspects of the line and of Lily's vision exist only as she holds them in her mind in the "second" it takes to complete her painting. If there is an allusion in the novel to the "It is done." of the *Revelation* of St. John, it is surely ironic. Lily thinks, "It was done . . . I have had my vision," in a deliberate and significant past-tense expression, for in the instant she feels her vision as a moment of eternity it is over. Every vision must return to time, and every end be merely a new beginning.

In the final lines of *The Years* (1937), Eleanor Pargiter has a similar moment of vision but the open-ended nature of the process is made more clear:

> She held her hands hollowed; she felt that she wanted to enclose the present moment; to make it stay; to fill it fuller and fuller, with the past, the present and the future, until it shone, whole, bright, deep with understanding.
>
> "Edward," she began, trying to attract his attention. But he was not listening. . . . It's useless, she thought, opening her hands. It must drop. It must fall. And then? she thought.

When she died, Virginia Woolf left behind the manuscript of a new novel (*Between the Acts*), the last words of which are "Then the curtain rose. They spoke." It is as impossible to separate the sense of "end" in her novels as it is to freeze the fullness of a wave at its crest into a static form. What is constant is the rhythm itself and the potential form which underlies and shapes each new surge of water: "So on

a summer's day waves collect, overbalance, and fall; collect and fall;
and the whole world seems to be saying 'that is all.' " (*Mrs. Dalloway*)
Numerous critics have remarked that it is all very well to be impressed
by Virginia Woolf's gift for language and undeniable skill in evoking
the streamy flux of life, but that at the end we are left only with the
banal notion that only change is unchanging. There is a difference
however between the banality of an idea or concept, and the felt sense
of the innermost rhythm of life, an internalized form like that left
by music, rather than an idea to be discussed and forgotten or a picture to be hung in the attics. Such a form can never be completed.

Another day; another Friday; another twentieth of March, January, or
September. Another general awakening. The stars draw back and are
extinguished. The bars deepen themselves between the waves. The film
of mist thickens on the fields. A redness gathers on the roses, even on
the pale rose that hangs by the bedroom window. A bird chirps. Cot-
tagers light their early candles. Yes, this is the eternal renewal, the
incessant rise and fall and fall and rise again. (Bernard in *The Waves*)

PART ONE

Interpretations

The Brown Stocking

by Erich Auerbach

This piece of narrative prose is the fifth section of part 1 in Virginia Woolf's novel, *To the Lighthouse,* which was first published in 1927. The situation in which the characters find themselves can be almost completely deduced from the text itself. Nowhere in the novel is it set forth systematically, by way of introduction or exposition, or in any other way than as it is here. I shall, however, briefly summarize what the situation is at the beginning of our passage. This will make it easier for the reader to understand the following analysis; it will also serve to bring out more clearly a number of important motifs from earlier sections which are here only alluded to.

Mrs. Ramsay is the wife of an eminent London professor of philosophy; she is very beautiful but definitely no longer young. With her youngest son James—he is six years old—she is sitting by the window in a good-sized summer house on one of the Hebrides islands. The professor has rented it for many years. In addition to the Ramsays, their eight children, and the servants, there are a number of guests in the house, friends on longer or shorter visits. Among them is a well-known botanist, William Bankes, an elderly widower, and Lily Briscoe, who is a painter. These two are just passing by the window. James is sitting on the floor busily cutting pictures from an illustrated catalogue. Shortly before, his mother had told him that, if the weather should be fine, they would sail to the lighthouse the next day. This is an expedition James had been looking forward to for a long time. The people at the lighthouse are to receive various presents; among these

"The Brown Stocking." From Mimesis: The Representation of Reality in Western Literature *by Erich Auerbach, trans. by Willard R. Trask (Princeton, N.J.: Princeton University Press [Princeton Paperback], 1968), pp. 463–78, 487–88. Copyright 1953 by Princeton University Press. Reprinted by permission of the publisher. The editor has omitted the beginning of the chapter, which is a full quotation of Part I, Section V of the novel, and nine pages which compare Woolf's technique with Proust and Joyce.*

are stockings for the lighthouse-keeper's boy. The violent joy which James had felt when the trip was announced had been as violently cut short by his father's acid observation that the weather would not be fine the next day. One of the guests, with malicious emphasis, has added some corroborative meteorological details. After all the others have left the room, Mrs. Ramsay, to console James, speaks the words with which our passage opens.

The continuity of the section is established through an exterior occurrence involving Mrs. Ramsay and James: the measuring of the stocking. Immediately after her consoling words (if it isn't fine tomorrow, we'll go some other day), Mrs. Ramsay makes James stand up so that she can measure the stocking for the lighthouse-keeper's son against his leg. A little further on she rather absent-mindedly tells him to stand still—the boy is fidgeting because his jealousy makes him a little stubborn and perhaps also because he is still under the impression of the disappointment of a few moments ago. Many lines later, the warning to stand still is repeated more sharply. James obeys, the measuring takes place, and it is found that the stocking is still considerably too short. After another long interval the scene concludes with Mrs. Ramsay kissing the boy on the forehead (she thus makes up for the sharp tone of her second order to him to stand still) and her proposing to help him look for another picture to cut out. Here the section ends.

This entirely insignificant occurrence is constantly interspersed with other elements which, although they do not interrupt its progress, take up far more time in the narration than the whole scene can possibly have lasted. Most of these elements are inner processes, that is, movements within the consciousness of individual personages, and not necessarily of personages involved in the exterior occurrence but also of others who are not even present at the time: "people," or "Mr. Bankes." In addition other exterior occurrences which might be called secondary and which pertain to quite different times and places (the telephone conversation, the construction of the building, for example) are worked in and made to serve as the frame for what goes on in the consciousness of third persons. Let us examine this in detail.

Mrs. Ramsay's very first remark is twice interrupted: first by the visual impression she receives of William Bankes and Lily Briscoe passing by together, and then, after a few intervening words serving the progress of the exterior occurrence, by the impression which the two persons passing by have left in her: the charm of Lily's Chinese eyes, which it is not for every man to see—whereupon she finishes her sentence and also allows her consciousness to dwell for a moment on the measuring of the stocking: we may yet go to the lighthouse, and so I must make sure the stocking is long enough. At this point there flashes into her mind the idea which has been prepared by her reflection on Lily's Chinese eyes (William and Lily ought to marry)—an admirable idea, she loves making matches. Smiling, she begins measuring the stocking. But the boy, in his stubborn and jealous love of her, refuses to stand still. How can she see whether the stocking is the right length if the boy keeps fidgeting about? What is the matter with James, her youngest, her darling? She looks up. Her eye falls on the room—and a long parenthesis begins. From the shabby chairs of which Andrew, her eldest son, said the other day that their entrails were all over the floor, her thoughts wander on, probing the objects and the people of her environment. The shabby furniture . . . but still good enough for up here; the advantages of the summer place; so cheap, so good for the children, for her husband; easily fitted up with a few old pieces of furniture, some pictures and books. Books—it is ages since she has had time to read books, even the books which have been dedicated to her (here the lighthouse flashes in for a second, as a place where one can't send such erudite volumes as some of those lying about the room). Then the house again: if the family would only be a little more careful. But of course, Andrew brings in crabs he wants to dissect; the other children gather seaweed, shells, stones; and she has to let them. All the children are gifted, each in a different way. But naturally, the house gets shabbier as a result (here the parenthesis is interrupted for a moment; she holds the stocking against James's leg); everything goes to ruin. If only the doors weren't always left open. See, everything is getting spoiled, even that Cashmere shawl on the picture frame. The doors are always left open; they are open again now. She listens: Yes, they are all open. The window on the landing is open too; she opened it herself. Windows must be open, doors closed. Why is it that no one can get that into his head? If you go to the maids' rooms at night, you will find all the windows closed. Only the Swiss maid always keeps her window open. She needs fresh air. Yesterday she looked out of the window with tears in her eyes and said: At home the mountains are so beautiful. Mrs. Ramsay knew that "at home" the girl's father was dying. Mrs. Ramsay had just been trying to teach her how to make beds, how to open windows. She had been talking away and had scolded the girl too. But then she had stopped talking (comparison with a bird folding its wings after flying in sunlight). She had stopped talking, for there was nothing one could say; he has cancer of the throat. At this point, remembering how she had stood there, how the girl had said at home the mountains were so beautiful—and there was no hope left—a sudden tense exasperation arises in her (exasperation with the cruel meaninglessness of a life whose continuance she is nevertheless striving with all her powers to abet, support, and secure). Her exasperation flows out into the exterior action. The parenthesis suddenly closes (it cannot have taken up more than a few seconds; just now she was still smiling over the thought of a marriage between Mr. Bankes and Lily Briscoe), and she says sharply to James: Stand still. Don't be so tiresome.

This is the first major parenthesis. The second starts a little later, after the stocking has been measured and found to be still much too short. It starts with the paragraph which begins and ends with the motif, "never did anybody look so sad."

Who is speaking in this paragraph? Who is looking at Mrs. Ramsay here, who concludes that never did anybody look so sad? Who is expressing these doubtful, obscure suppositions?—about the tear which —perhaps—forms and falls in the dark, about the water swaying this way and that, receiving it, and then returning to rest? There is no one near the window in the room but Mrs. Ramsay and James. It cannot be either of them, nor the "people" who begin to speak in the next paragraph. Perhaps it is the author. However, if that be so, the author certainly does not speak like one who has a knowledge of his characters—in this case, of Mrs. Ramsay—and who, out of his knowledge, can describe their personality and momentary state of mind objectively and with certainty. Virginia Woolf wrote this paragraph. She did not identify it through grammatical and typographical devices as the speech or thought of a third person. One is obliged to assume that it contains direct statements of her own. But she does not seem to bear in mind that she is the author and hence ought to know how matters stand with her characters. The person speaking here, whoever it is, acts the part of one who has only an impression of Mrs. Ramsay, who looks at her face and renders the impression received, but is doubtful of its proper interpretation. "Never did anybody look so sad" is not an objective statement. In rendering the shock received by one looking at Mrs. Ramsay's face, it verges upon a realm beyond reality. And in the ensuing passage the speakers no longer seem to be human beings at all but spirits between heaven and earth, nameless spirits capable of penetrating the depths of the human soul, capable too of knowing something about it, but not of attaining clarity as to what is in process there, with the result that what they report has a doubtful ring, comparable in a way to those "certain airs, detached from the body of the wind," which in a later passage (2, 2) move about the house at night, "questioning and wondering." However that may be, here too we are not dealing with objective utterances on the part of the author in respect to one of the characters. No one is certain of anything here: it is all mere supposition, glances cast by one person upon another whose enigma he cannot solve.

This continues in the following paragraph. Suppositions as to the meaning of Mrs. Ramsay's expression are made and discussed. But the level of tone descends slightly, from the poetic and non-real to the practical and earthly; and now a speaker is introduced: "People said." People wonder whether some recollection of an unhappy occurrence in her earlier life is hidden behind her radiant beauty. There have been rumors to that effect. But perhaps the rumors are wrong: nothing of this is to be learned directly from her; she is silent when such things come up in conversation. But supposing she has never experienced anything of the sort herself, she yet knows everything even without experience. The simplicity and genuineness of her being unfailingly light upon the truth of things, and, falsely perhaps, delight, ease, sustain.

Is it still "people" who are speaking here? We might almost be tempted to doubt it, for the last words sound almost too personal and thoughtful for the gossip of "people." And immediately afterward, suddenly and unexpectedly, an entirely new speaker, a new scene, and a new time are introduced. We find Mr. Bankes at the telephone talking to Mrs. Ramsay, who has called him to tell him about a train connection, evidently with reference to a journey they are planning to make together. The paragraph about the tear had already taken us out of the room where Mrs. Ramsay and James are sitting by the window; it had transported us to an undefinable scene beyond the realm of reality. The paragraph in which the rumors are discussed has a concretely earthly but not clearly identified scene. Now we find ourselves in a precisely determined place, but far away from the summer house—in London, in Mr. Bankes's house. The time is not stated ("once"), but apparently the telephone conversation took place long (perhaps as much as several years) before this particular sojourn in the house on the island. But what Mr. Bankes says over the telephone is in perfect continuity with the preceding paragraph. Again not objectively but in the form of the impression received by a specific person at a specific moment, it as it were sums up all that precedes— the scene with the Swiss maid, the hidden sadness in Mrs. Ramsay's beautiful face, what people think about her, and the impression she makes: Nature has but little clay like that of which she molded her. Did Mr. Bankes really say that to her over the telephone? Or did he only want to say it when he heard her voice, which moved him deeply, and it came into his mind how strange it was to be talking over the telephone with this wonderful woman, so like a Greek goddess? The sentence is enclosed in quotation marks, so one would suppose that he really spoke it. But this is not certain, for the first words of his soliloquy, which follows, are likewise enclosed in quotation marks. In any case, he quickly gets hold of himself, for he answers in a matter-of-fact way that he will catch the 10:30 at Euston.

But his emotion does not die away so quickly. As he puts down the

receiver and walks across the room to the window in order to watch
the work on a new building across the way—apparently his usual and
characteristic procedure when he wants to relax and let his thoughts
wander freely—he continues to be preoccupied with Mrs. Ramsay.
There is always something strange about her, something that does
not quite go with her beauty (as for instance telephoning); she has no
awareness of her beauty, or at most only a childish awareness; her
dress and her actions show that at times. She is constantly getting
involved in everyday realities which are hard to reconcile with the
harmony of her face. In his methodical way he tries to explain her
incongruities to himself. He puts forward some conjectures but cannot make up his mind. Meanwhile his momentary impressions of the
work on the new building keep crowding in. Finally he gives it up.
With the somewhat impatient, determined matter-of-factness of a
methodical and scientific worker (which he is) he shakes off the in-
soluble problem "Mrs. Ramsay." He knows no solution (the repetition
of "he did not know" symbolizes his impatient shaking it off). He has
to get back to his work.

Here the second long interruption comes to an end and we are
taken back to the room where Mrs. Ramsay and James are. The exterior occurrence is brought to a close with the kiss on James's forehead and the resumption of the cutting out of pictures. But here
too we have only an exterior change. A scene previously abandoned
reappears, suddenly and with as little transition as if it had never
been left, as though the long interruption were only a glance which
someone (who?) has cast from it into the depths of time. But the
theme (Mrs. Ramsay, her beauty, the enigma of her character, her
absoluteness, which nevertheless always exercises itself in the relativity
and ambiguity of life, in what does not become her beauty) carries
over directly from the last phase of the interruption (that is, Mr.
Bankes's fruitless reflections) into the situation in which we now find
Mrs. Ramsay: "with her head outlined absurdly by the gilt frame"
etc.—for once again what is around her is not suited to her, is "something incongruous." And the kiss she gives her little boy, the words
she speaks to him, although they are a genuine gift of life, which
James accepts as the most natural and simple truth, are yet heavy
with unsolved mystery.

Our analysis of the passage yields a number of distinguishing stylistic
characteristics, which we shall now attempt to formulate.

The writer as narrator of objective facts has almost completely
vanished; almost everything stated appears by way of reflection in the
consciousness of the dramatis personae. When it is a question of the
house, for example, or of the Swiss maid, we are not given the objective
information which Virginia Woolf possesses regarding these objects of

her creative imagination but what Mrs. Ramsay thinks or feels about
them at a particular moment. Similarly we are not taken into Virginia
Woolf's confidence and allowed to share her knowledge of Mrs. Ramsay's character; we are given her character as it is reflected in and as
it affects various figures in the novel: the nameless spirits which
assume certain things about a tear, the people who wonder about her,
and Mr. Bankes. In our passage this goes so far that there actually
seems to be no viewpoint at all outside the novel from which the
people and events within it are observed, any more than there seems
to be an objective reality apart from what is in the consciousness of
the characters. Remnants of such a reality survive at best in brief
references to the exterior frame of the action, such as "said Mrs.
Ramsay, raising her eyes . . ." or "said Mr. Bankes once, hearing her
voice." The last paragraph ("Knitting her reddish-brown hairy stocking . . .") might perhaps also be mentioned in this connection. But
this is already somewhat doubtful. The occurrence is described objectively, but as for its interpretation, the tone indicates that the
author looks at Mrs. Ramsay not with knowing but with doubting
and questioning eyes—even as some character in the novel would see
her in the situation in which she is described, would hear her speak
the words given.

The devices employed in this instance (and by a number of contemporary writers as well) to express the contents of the consciousness
of the dramatis personae have been analyzed and described syntacti-
cally. Some of them have been named (*erlebte Rede,* stream of consciousness, *monologue intérieur* are examples). Yet these stylistic forms,
especially the *erlebte Rede,* were used in literature much earlier too,
but not for the same aesthetic purpose. And in addition to them there
are other possibilities—hardly definable in terms of syntax—of obscur-
ing and even obliterating the impression of an objective reality completely known to the author; possibilities, that is, dependent not on
form but on intonation and context. A case in point is the passage under discussion, where the author at times achieves the intended effect
by representing herself to be someone who doubts, wonders, hesitates,
as though the truth about her characters were not better known to her
than it is to them or to the reader. It is all, then, a matter of the
author's attitude toward the reality of the world he represents. And
this attitude differs entirely from that of authors who interpret the
actions, situations, and characters of their personages with objective
assurance, as was the general practice in earlier times. Goethe or
Keller, Dickens or Meredith, Balzac or Zola told us out of their certain
knowledge what their characters did, what they felt and thought while
doing it, and how their actions and thoughts were to be interpreted.
They knew everything about their characters. To be sure, in past

periods too we were frequently told about the subjective reactions of
the characters in a novel or story; at times even in the form of *erlebte
Rede,* although more frequently as a monologue, and of course in
most instances with an introductory phrase something like "it seemed
to him that . . ." or "at this moment he felt that . . ." or the like.
Yet in such cases there was hardly ever any attempt to render the flow
and the play of consciousness adrift in the current of changing impressions (as is done in our text both for Mrs. Ramsay and for Mr.
Bankes); instead, the content of the individual's consciousness was
rationally limited to things connected with the particular incident
being related or the particular situation being described—as is the
case, for example, in the passage from *Madame Bovary* interpreted
above (pp. 425ff.). And what is still more important: the author, with
his knowledge of an objective truth, never abdicated his position as the
final and governing authority. Again, earlier writers, especially from
the end of the nineteenth century on, had produced narrative works
which on the whole undertook to give us an extremely subjective,
individualistic, and often eccentrically aberrant impression of reality,
and which neither sought nor were able to ascertain anything objective
or generally valid in regard to it. Sometimes such works took the
form of first-person novels; sometimes they did not. As an example of
the latter case I mention Huysmans's novel *A rebours.* But all that
too is basically different from the modern procedure here described on
the basis of Virginia Woolf's text, although the latter, it is true,
evolved from the former. The essential characteristic of the technique
represented by Virginia Woolf is that we are given not merely one
person whose consciousness (that is, the impressions it receives) is
rendered, but many persons, with frequent shifts from one to the
other—in our text, Mrs. Ramsay, "people," Mr. Bankes, in brief
interludes James, the Swiss maid in a flash-back, and the nameless
ones who speculate over a tear. The multiplicity of persons suggests
that we are here after all confronted with an endeavor to investigate
an objective reality, that is, specifically, the "real" Mrs. Ramsay. She
is, to be sure, an enigma and such she basically remains, but she is as
it were encircled by the content of all the various consciousnesses
directed upon her (including her own); there is an attempt to approach her from many sides as closely as human possibilities of perception and expression can succeed in doing. The design of a close
approach to objective reality by means of numerous subjective impressions received by various individuals (and at various times) is important in the modern technique which we are here examining. It
basically differentiates it from the unipersonal subjectivism which allows only a single and generally a very unusual person to make himself
heard and admits only that one person's way of looking at reality.

In terms of literary history, to be sure, there are close connections between the two methods of representing consciousness—the unipersonal subjective method and the multipersonal method with synthesis as its aim. The latter developed from the former, and there are works in which the two overlap, so that we can watch the development. This is especially the case in Marcel Proust's great novel. We shall return to it later.

Another stylistic peculiarity to be observed in our text—though one that is closely and necessarily connected with the "multipersonal representation of consciousness" just discussed—has to do with the treatment of time. That there is something peculiar about the treatment of time in modern narrative literature is nothing new; several studies have been published on the subject. These were primarily attempts to establish a connection between the pertinent phenomena and contemporary philosophical doctrines or trends—undoubtedly a justifiable undertaking and useful for an appreciation of the community of interests and inner purposes shown in the activity of many of our contemporaries. We shall begin by describing the procedure with reference to our present example. We remarked earlier that the act of measuring the length of the stocking and the speaking of the words related to it must have taken much less time than an attentive reader who tries not to miss anything will require to read the passage— even if we assume that a brief pause intervened between the measuring and the kiss of reconciliation on James's forehead. However, the time the narration takes is not devoted to the occurrence itself (which is rendered rather tersely) but to interludes. Two long excursuses are inserted, whose relations in time to the occurrence which frames them seem to be entirely different. The first excursus, a representation of what goes on in Mrs. Ramsay's mind while she measures the stocking (more precisely, between the first absent-minded and the second sharp order to James to hold his leg still) belongs in time to the framing occurrence, and it is only the representation of it which takes a greater number of seconds and even minutes than the measuring—the reason being that the road taken by consciousness is sometimes traversed far more quickly than language is able to render it, if we want to make ourselves intelligible to a third person, and that is the intention here. What goes on in Mrs. Ramsay's mind in itself contains nothing enigmatic; these are ideas which arise from her daily life and may well be called normal—her secret lies deeper, and it is only when the switch from the open windows to the Swiss maid's words comes, that something happens which lifts the veil a little. On the whole, however, the mirroring of Mrs. Ramsay's consciousness is much more easily comprehensible than the sort of thing we get in such cases from other authors (James Joyce, for example). But simple and trivial as are the ideas which arise one after the other in Mrs. Ramsay's consciousness, they are at the same time essential and significant. They amount to a synthesis of the intricacies of life in which her incomparable beauty has been caught, in which it at once manifests and conceals itself. Of course, writers of earlier periods too occasionally devoted some time and a few sentences to telling the reader what at a specific moment passed through their characters' minds—but for such a purpose they would hardly have chosen so accidental an occasion as Mrs. Ramsay's looking up, so that, quite involuntarily, her eyes fall on the furniture. Nor would it have occurred to them to render the continuous rumination of consciousness in its natural and purposeless freedom. And finally they would not have inserted the entire process between two exterior occurrences so close together in time as the two warnings to James to keep still (both of which, after all, take place while she is on the point of holding the unfinished stocking to his leg); so that, in a surprising fashion unknown to earlier periods, a sharp contrast results between the brief span of time occupied by the exterior event and the dreamlike wealth of a process of consciousness which traverses a whole subjective universe. These are the characteristic and distinctively new features of the technique: a chance occasion releasing processes of consciousness; a natural and even, if you will, a naturalistic rendering of those processes in their peculiar freedom, which is neither restrained by a purpose nor directed by a specific subject of thought; elaboration of the contrast between "exterior" and "interior" time. The three have in common what they reveal of the author's attitude: he submits, much more than was done in earlier realistic works, to the random contingency of real phenomena; and even though he winnows and stylizes the material of the real world—as of course he cannot help doing—he does not proceed rationalistically, nor with a view to bringing a continuity of exterior events to a planned conclusion. In Virginia Woolf's case the exterior events have actually lost their hegemony, they serve to release and interpret inner events, whereas before her time (and still today in many instances) inner movements preponderantly function to prepare and motivate significant exterior happenings. This too is apparent in the randomness and contingency of the exterior occasion (looking up because James does not keep his foot still), which releases the much more significant inner process.

The temporal relation between the second excursus and the framing occurrence is of a different sort: its content (the passage on the tear, the things people think about Mrs. Ramsay, the telephone conversation with Mr. Bankes and his reflections while watching the building of the new hotel) is not a part of the framing occurrence either in terms of time or of place. Other times and places are in question; it is an excursus of the same type as the story of the origin of Odysseus' scar, which was discussed in the first chapter of this book. Even from that, however, it is different in structure. In the Homer passage the excursus was linked to the scar which Euryclea touches with her hands, and although the moment in which the touching of the scar occurs is one of high and dramatic tension, the scene nevertheless immediately shifts to another clear and luminous present, and this present seems actually designed to cut off the dramatic tension and cause the entire footwashing scene to be temporarily forgotten. In Virginia Woolf's passage, there is no question of any tension. Nothing of importance in a dramatic sense takes place; the problem is the length of the stocking. The point of departure for the excursus is Mrs. Ramsay's facial expression: "never did anybody look so sad." In fact several excursuses start from here; three, to be exact. And all three differ in time and place, differ too in definiteness of time and place, the first being situated quite vaguely, the second somewhat more definitely, and the third with comparative precision. Yet none of them is so exactly situated in time as the successive episodes of the story of Odysseus' youth, for even in the case of the telephone scene we have only an inexact indication of when it occurred. As a result it becomes possible to accomplish the shifting of the scene away from the windownook much more unnoticeably and smoothly than the changing of scene and time in the episode of the scar. In the passage on the tear the reader may still be in doubt as to whether there has been any shift at all. The nameless speakers may have entered the room and be looking at Mrs. Ramsay. In the second paragraph this interpretation is no longer possible, but the "people" whose gossip is reproduced are still looking at Mrs. Ramsay's face—not here and now, at the summer-house window, but it is still the same face and has the same expression. And even in the third part, where the face is no longer physically seen (for Mr. Bankes is talking to Mrs. Ramsay over the telephone), it is nonetheless present to his inner vision; so that not for an instant does the theme (the solution of the enigma Mrs. Ramsay), and even the moment when the problem is formulated (the expression of her face while she measures the length of the stocking), vanish from the reader's memory. In terms of the exterior event the three parts of the excursus have nothing to do with one another. They have no common and externally coherent development, as have the episodes of Odysseus' youth which are related with reference to the origin of the scar; they are connected only by the one thing they have in common—looking at Mrs. Ramsay, and more specifically at the Mrs. Ramsay who, with an unfathomable expression of sadness behind her radiant beauty, concludes that the stocking is still much too short. It is only this common focus which connects the otherwise totally different parts of the excursus; but the connection is strong enough to deprive them of the independent "present" which the episode of the scar possesses. They are nothing but attempts to interpret "never did anybody look so sad"; they carry on this theme, which itself carries on after they conclude: there has been no change of theme at all. In contrast, the scene in which Euryclea recognizes Odysseus is interrupted and divided into two parts by the excursus on the origin of the scar. In our passage, there is no such clear distinction between two exterior occurrences and between two presents. However insignificant as an exterior event the framing occurrence (the measuring of the stocking) may be, the picture of Mrs. Ramsay's face which arises from it remains present throughout the excursus; the excursus itself is nothing but a background for that picture, which seems as it were to open into the depths of time—just as the first excursus, released by Mr. Ramsay's unintentional glance at the furniture, was an opening of the picture into the depths of consciousness.

The two excursuses, then, are not as different as they at first appeared. It is not so very important that the first, so far as time is concerned (and place too), runs its course within the framing occurrence, while the second conjures up other times and places. The times and places of the second are not independent; they serve only the polyphonic treatment of the image which releases it; as a matter of fact, they impress us (as does the interior time of the first excursus) like an occurrence in the consciousness of some observer (to be sure, he is not identified) who might see Mrs. Ramsay at the described moment and whose meditation upon the unsolved enigma of her personality might contain memories of what others (people, Mr. Bankes) say and think about her. In both excursuses we are dealing with attempts to fathom a more genuine, a deeper, and indeed a more real reality; in both cases the incident which releases the excursus appears accidental and is poor in content; in both cases it makes little difference whether the excursuses employ only the consciousness-content, and hence only interior time, or whether they also employ exterior shifts of time. After all, the process of consciousness in the first excursus likewise includes shifts of time and scene, especially the episode with the Swiss maid. The important point is that an insignificant exterior occurrence releases ideas and chains of ideas which cut loose from the present of the exterior occurrence and range freely through the depths of time. It is as though an apparently simple text revealed its proper content only in the commentary on it, a simple musical theme only in the development-section. This enables us also to understand the close relation between the treatment of time and the "multipersonal representation of consciousness" discussed earlier. The ideas arising in consciousness are not tied to the present of the exterior occurrence which releases them. Virginia Woolf's peculiar technique, as exemplified in our text, consists in the fact that the exterior objective reality of the momentary present which the author directly reports and which appears as established fact—in our instance the measuring of the stocking—is nothing but an occasion (although perhaps not an entirely accidental one). The stress is placed entirely on what the occasion releases, things which are not seen directly but by reflection, which are not tied to the present of the framing occurrence which realeases them.

. . . Let us turn again to the text which was our starting-point. It breathes an air of vague and hopeless sadness. We never come to learn what Mrs. Ramsay's situation really is. Only the sadness, the vanity of her beauty and vital force emerge from the depths of secrecy. Even when we have read the whole novel, the meaning of the relationship between the planned trip to the lighthouse and the actual trip many years later remains unexpressed, enigmatic, only dimly to be conjectured, as does the content of Lily Briscoe's concluding vision which enables her to finish her painting with one stroke of the brush. It is one of the few books of this type which are filled with good and genuine love but also, in its feminine way, with irony, amorphous sadness, and doubt of life. Yet what realistic depth is achieved in every individual occurrence, for example the measuring of the stocking! Aspects of the occurrence come to the fore, and links to other occurrences, which, before this time, had hardly been sensed, which had never been clearly seen and attended to, and yet they are determining factors in our real lives. What takes place here in Virginia Woolf's novel is precisely what was attempted everywhere in works of this kind (although not everywhere with the same insight and mastery)— that is, to put the emphasis on the random occurrence, to exploit it not in the service of a planned continuity of action but in itself. And in the process something new and elemental appeared: nothing less than the wealth of reality and depth of life in every moment to which we surrender ourselves without prejudice. To be sure, what happens in that moment—be it outer or inner processes—concerns in a very personal way the individuals who live in it, but it also (and for that very reason) concerns the elementary things which men in general have in common. It is precisely the random moment which is comparatively independent of the controversial and unstable orders over which men fight and despair; it passes unaffected by them, as daily life. The more it is exploited, the more the elementary things which our lives have in common come to light. The more numerous, varied, and simple the people are who appear as subjects of such random moments, the more effectively must what they have in common shine forth. In this unprejudiced and exploratory type of representation we cannot but see to what an extent—below the surface conflicts—the differences between men's ways of life and forms of thought have already lessened. The strata of societies and their different ways of life have become inextricably mingled. There are no longer even exotic peoples. A century ago (in Mérimée for example), Corsicans or Spaniards were still exotic; today the term would be quite unsuitable for Pearl Buck's Chinese peasants. Beneath the conflicts, and also through them, an economic and cultural leveling process is taking place. It is still a long way to a common life of mankind on earth, but the goal begins to be visible. And it is most concretely visible now in the unprejudiced, precise, interior and exterior representation of the random moment in the lives of different people. So the complicated process of dissolution which led to fragmentation of the exterior action, to reflection of consciousness, and to stratification of time seems to be tending toward a very simple solution. Perhaps it will be too simple to please those who, despite all its dangers and catastrophes, admire and love our epoch for the sake of its abundance of life and the incomparable historical vantage point which it affords. But they are few in number, and probably they will not live to see much more than the first forewarnings of the approaching unification and simplification.

To the Lighthouse

by A. D. Moody

Part II, as its title "Time Passes" suggests, enforces and explores the facts of transience and death. If the human energies and aspirations expressed in the character of Mrs. Ramsay can be thought of as the novel's thesis, then the processes of nature are here set against them as their antithesis. They are realised directly, not through the filter of a human consciousness as in the rest of the novel. In consequence the world of mind is placed for the moment in the diminishing perspectives of the external world, and its visions are exposed to the indifference of physical nature.

Two passages will serve to bring out the main points. They are concerned with the relation to the natural order of the human desire for stability and order, and examine in particular the appearances of the external world which seem to support Mrs. Ramsay's vision of an enduring and immune perfection.

> As summer neared, as the evenings lengthened, there came to the wakeful, the hopeful, walking the beach, stirring the pool, imaginations of the strangest kind—of flesh turned to atoms which drove before the wind, of stars flashing in their hearts, of cliff, sea, cloud, and sky brought purposely together to assemble outwardly the scattered parts of the vision within. In those mirrors, the minds of men, in those pools of uneasy water, in which clouds for ever turn and shadows form, dreams persisted, and it was impossible to resist the strange intimation which every gull, flower, tree, man and woman, and the white earth itself seemed to declare (but if questioned at once to withdraw) that good triumphs, happiness prevails, order rules; or to resist the extraordinary stimulus to range hither and thither in search of some absolute good, some crystal of intensity, remote from the known pleasures and familiar virtues, something alien to the processes of domestic life, single, hard, bright, like a diamond in the sand, which would render the possessor secure.[1]

"To the Lighthouse." *From* Virginia Woolf *by A. D. Moody.* (*Edinburgh: Oliver and Boyd Limited, 1963*), *pp. 36–43. Reprinted by permission of the publisher.*

[1] *L.,* pp. 204–5.

That aspiration is placed against such facts as Prue Ramsay's dying in childbirth, Andrew's being killed in the War, and Mrs. Ramsay's death: the cold facts of human experience deny the dream. There are moreover the brute processes of nature, whereby weeds grow over the windows, and the abandoned house falls into decay. The only conclusion to be drawn is this:

> Did Nature supplement what man advanced? Did she complete what he began? With equal complacence she saw his misery, condoned his meanness, and acquiesced in his torture. That dream, then, of sharing, completing, finding in solitude on the beach an answer, was but a reflection in a mirror, and the mirror itself was but the surface glassiness which forms in quiescence when the nobler powers sleep beneath? Impatient, despairing yet loth to go (for beauty offers her lures, has her consolations), to pace the beach was impossible; contemplation was unendurable; the mirror was broken.[2]

This is not a conclusion of despair—the weight of the novel's aspirations have not, after all, been rested upon nature. The point is rather that, since the desired human order has no sanction or support in the external world, the responsibility for creating and sustaining it is thrown back upon man himself, and his nobler powers are summoned to action.

That had been Mrs. Ramsay's response—a more determined effort to promote human relationships and individual fulfilment. But her efforts had seemed to be brought to nothing by her death. In Part III, "The Lighthouse," this appearance is refuted by an intensive demonstration of her persisting power. What she had achieved in her life continues to fructify in the lives of her children, and in the mind and art of Lily Briscoe. The latter especially complements and continues Mrs. Ramsay's achievements, in the other sphere of art, and, under her inspiration, reaches towards the complete vision she had sought.

In her painting Lily is working at the problem of relating two opposed masses, and resolving them into a unified image. But while her mind works at that it works also at the problem of comprehending the Ramsays. Her abstract aesthetic problem becomes an analogy for her main concern, and the novel's, which is to bring Mr. and Mrs. Ramsay, and the worlds they represent, into a harmonious relation. Her progress with her painting marks the stages of a progression towards that achievement.

In the early sections of Part III Lily's inadequacies in ordinary human relationships are markedly contrasted with Mrs. Ramsay's gifts. But then, in her complementary activity, she is shown doing almost exactly what Mrs. Ramsay had done in Part I. As she begins

[2] *L.,* pp. 207-8.

her picture she exchanges "the fluidity of life for the concentration of painting";[3] and her pursuit of "this other thing, this truth, this reality" at the back of appearances, while it parallels Mrs. Ramsay's, is equally counteracted by the insistent demands of ordinary and actual experience.

For the most part she is engaged in recalling and celebrating Mrs. Ramsay; and her thinking about her amounts to a re-enactment of her life, which brings a clearer understanding of her achievements. But what emerges most clearly is that Mrs. Ramsay is not simply the object of her contemplation, but is in the fullest sense her inspiration. And the force of her inspiration for Lily's vision is what her active influence had been in life:

> [she] resolved everything into simplicity; made these angers, irritations fall off like old rags; she brought together this and that and then this, and so made out of that miserable silliness and spite (she and Charles squabbling, sparring, had been silly and spiteful) something—this scene on the beach for example, this moment of friendship and liking—which survived, after all these years, complete, so that she dipped into it to re-fashion her memory of him, and it stayed in the mind almost like a work of art.[4]

What Mrs. Ramsay had been in her life provides an answer then to Lily's questioning of life, and reveals how a human order may be established within the flux of nature:

> What is the meaning of life? That was all—a simple question; one that tended to close in on one with years. The great revelation had never come. The great revelation perhaps never did come. Instead there were little daily miracles, illuminations, matches struck unexpectedly in the dark; here was one. This, that, and the other; herself and Charles Tansley and the breaking wave; Mrs. Ramsay bringing them together; Mrs. Ramsay saying "Life stand still here"; Mrs. Ramsay making of the moment something permanent (as in another sphere Lily herself tried to make of the moment something permanent)—this was of the nature of a revelation. In the midst of chaos there was shape; this eternal passing and flowing (she looked at the clouds going and the leaves shaking) was struck into stability.[5]

That revelation is part of Lily Briscoe's vision, and the main and most satisfying part. But it is not complete in itself. Having satisfied her sense of Mrs. Ramsay she becomes aware of a need to comprehend Mr. Ramsay as well, and to be on a level with ordinary experience.[6]

[3] *L.*, p. 245; cp. pp. 99–102, 162–3.

[4] *L.*, pp. 248–9.

[5] *L.*, pp. 249–50.

[6] cp. *L.*, p. 310.

Her concern with Mrs. Ramsay has been counterpointed throughout by Mr. Ramsay's demands upon her notice, and by the account of his crossing to the lighthouse. She had felt that he threatened ruin and chaos to her vision: but his insistent presence remains to the same effect as the details of ordinary activity in Mrs. Ramsay's vision. Mrs. Ramsay's final triumph in life had been to acknowledge the truth of her husband's facts, and to make the acknowledgment an expression of love, so that their differences were resolved.[7] Lily Briscoe's painting, and the novel, are finally completed, and their vision achieved, by a similar acknowledgment and inclusion of him.

The key to the conclusion is the final stroke of Lily's painting, a line drawn in the centre, which relates and harmonises the opposed masses. The line suggests the lighthouse which Mr. Ramsay has just reached, and which, as its title implies, the whole novel has been approaching. The lighthouse, as the analogy of the line implies, has become the object in relation to which Mr. and Mrs. Ramsay's opposed views of reality have been comprehended and related. Several critics have tried to find some intrinsic symbolic meaning in the lighthouse, but without much success. It is hardly possible for it to be a symbol, at least in Coleridge's sense, of something which partakes of the reality which it represents. For a premise of Virginia Woolf's idea of the world is that there is no apprehensible ultimate reality which it could partake of and represent. In itself it is simply a light-house. Whatever further meanings it has come from what the characters make of it, by projecting onto it their different views of reality. In this way it gives to the novel a unifying focus for those views, but not a further "symbolic" perspective.

In Part I the lighthouse becomes identified with Mrs. Ramsay, and is made an image for her vision of "something immune which shines out." But she responds (and corresponds) only to the light, and leaves the actual structure out of account. In Part III the other view is approached as Mr. Ramsay sails across to it. Then it emerges as a stark tower on a bare rock, and is appropriately identified by James with Mr. Ramsay:

> He looked, James thought, getting his head now against the Lighthouse, now against the waste of waters running away into the open, like some old stone lying on the sand; he looked as if he had become physically what was always at the back of both of their minds—that loneliness which was for both of them the truth about things.[8]

At the beginning of the novel James had hated his father for insisting that the weather would prevent their going to the lighthouse. Now he

[7] cp. *L.*, pp. 190–1.
[8] *L.*, p. 311.

has changed, as the lighthouse itself has changed with their closer approach. He had thought of it in terms associated with his mother—"The Lighthouse was then a silvery, misty-looking tower with a yellow eye that opened suddenly and softly in the evening." Now he sees it "as it really is." But at the same time he perceives that both views are possible and true: "So that was the Lighthouse, was it? No, the other was also the Lighthouse. For nothing was simply one thing." [9]

In this way the lighthouse, and James himself, established Mr. Ramsay's rational reality, and Mrs. Ramsay's intuitive reality, in a relationship which admits the validity of both, and implies the necessity of both. At the same time the image defines their relative functions and values. Mr. Ramsay stands for the world of physical nature which is the element of human life, and for the science by which it is understood—for the stark tower on its bare rock above the chaos of the sea. But Mrs. Ramsay represents the spirit of life itself, the inward light which shines out, and is the essential energy creating and sustaining a distinctively human order. . . .

At the end then, as throughout the novel, there remain both the persistent division between the inner and external realities, and the exaltation of the former over the latter. The conclusion is something less than a resolution in the full sense. It is a relationship established almost entirely from the point of view of the intuitive imagination, and on the terms most to its advantage. It is symptomatic that the longer first and final parts of the novel are given over to the workings of that imagination, and that the chaotic energies of the natural world are abstracted and isolated in the brief middle section. Whatever reality is not subjected to the mind's processes is not allowed its due weight and effect. In consequence, with all its excellence as a work of art, the novel is rather limited to the sphere of art.

At the same time it is not a piece of art for art's sake aestheticism. The deliberate approach to the physical reality of the lighthouse rejects any temptation to make it an ivory tower. There is a consistent and strenuous attempt to relate the ideal to the actual, to accept life on the level of its necessary conditions, as well as on that of visionary aspiration. The attempt stops short of a final resolution of this divided and limiting view of life. But it is a considerable advance beyond the near absolute division obtaining in the earlier novels; and a step towards the more engaged and mature achievements of *The Waves* and *Between the Acts.*

[9] *L.,* p. 286.

The Semi-Transparent Envelope

by David Daiches

Two years after *Mrs. Dalloway* there appeared the book which marks the perfection of Virginia Woolf's art: *To the Lighthouse*. Here, instead of taking a group of characters in upper middle-class London society and wringing some rarified meaning out of their states of mind, she keeps her characters throughout the novel on an island in the Hebrides, an island unparticularized and remote, which, by its setting and associations, helps her to break down the apparent concreteness of character and events into that "luminous halo" which for her was the most adequate symbol of life. The basic plot framework is simple enough. The book is divided into three sections: the first "The Window," deals with Mr. and Mrs. Ramsay, their children and their guests on holiday on the island one late September day a few years before the first World War; the second, "Time Passes," gives an impressionist rendering of the change and decay which their house on the island suffers in the years following: the war prevents the family from revisiting the place, Mrs. Ramsay dies, Andrew Ramsay is killed in the war, Prue Ramsay dies in childbirth—all this is suggested parenthetically in the course of the account of the decay of the house; in the third and final section, "The Lighthouse," we see the remnant of the Ramsay family revisiting their house on the island some ten years later, with some of the same guests, and the book closes with Lily Briscoe, a guest on both visits, completing a picture she had begun on the first visit—completing it in the light of the vision which finally comes to her and enables her to see for a moment in their proper relation the true significance of the dead Mrs. Ramsay, of the whole Ramsay family, and of the physical scene in front of her. A further tie-up is effected in the actual visit to the lighthouse made by Mr. Ramsay and two of the children in the last section: this visit had been planned in the first section, but had been put off owing to bad weather, much to the disappointment of young James Ramsay and his mother, and so the visit, when it actually takes place years after Mrs. Ramsay's death, with James no longer a small boy but an adolescent, has a certain symbolic meaning. The arrival of the Ramsays at the lighthouse, and Lily Briscoe's achievement of her vision as she sits in front of the Ramsay's house painting and meditating, occur contemporaneously, and this conjunction possesses further symbolic significance.

Upon this framework Virginia Woolf weaves a delicate pattern of symbolic thoughts and situations. The book opens with a certain deliberate abruptness:

> "Yes, of course, if it's fine tomorrow," said Mrs. Ramsay. "But you'll have to be up with the lark," she added.

She is referring to the expedition to the lighthouse, on which young James, aged six, had set his heart. The planning and eventual accomplishment of this expedition constitute the main principle of integration employed by Virginia Woolf to unify the story. Following the opening remark of Mrs. Ramsay come James's reactions:

> To her son these words conveyed an extraordinary joy, as if it were settled, the expedition were bound to take place, and the wonder to which he had looked forward, for years and years it seemed, was, after a night's darkness and a day's sail, within touch. Since he belonged, even at the age of six, to that great clan which cannot keep this feeling separate from that, but must let future prospects, with their joys and sorrows, cloud what is actually at hand, since to such people even in earliest childhood any turn in the wheel of sensation has the power to crystallise and transfix the moment upon which its gloom or radiance rests, James Ramsay, sitting on the floor cutting out pictures from the illustrated catalogue of the Army and Navy Stores, endowed the picture of a refrigerator, as his mother spoke, with heavenly bliss. It was fringed with joy. The wheelbarrow, the lawnmower, the sound of poplar trees, leaves whitening before rain, rooks cawing, brooms knocking, dresses rustling— all these were so coloured and distinguished in his mind that he had already his private code, his secret language, though he appeared the image of stark and uncompromising severity, with his high forehead and his fierce blue eyes, impeccably candid and pure, frowning slightly at the sight of human frailty, so that his mother, watching him guide his scissors neatly round the refrigerator, imagined him all red and ermine on the Bench or directing a stern and momentous enterprise in some crisis of public affairs.

Here is a careful weaving together of character's consciousness, author's comment, and one character's view of another. On James's happy expectation crashes his father's ruthless remarks:

"But," said his father, stopping in front of the drawing-room window, "it won't be fine."

This remark arouses in James a fierce, frustrated anger. "Had there been an axe handy, or a poker, any weapon that would have gashed a hole in his father's breast and killed him, there and then, James would have seized it." Mr. Ramsay was always right, and James knew that his prophecy could not be laughed off. But his anger at his father's deliberate dashing of his hopes was increased rather than modified by this knowledge, and the grudge entered into his subconscious to be finally exorcised only when, ten years later, they arrive at the lighthouse and Mr. Ramsay turns and compliments James on his steering of the boat.

Virginia Woolf's handling of this point is, however, much subtler than this bald summary would suggest. For the theme is symbolic in its implications, and in her elaboration of it Virginia Woolf not only brings out the full character of James and his father, establishes their complex relation to each other, indicates the relation of Mr. Ramsay to the other characters and their relation to him, and illuminates some general problems concerning the relation of parents to children, husband to wife, and people to each other, but also endeavours to suggest indirectly certain profound ideas about experience and its dependence on time and personality. What is the most significant quality in experience? This is the question which *To the Lighthouse* seems designed to answer. In what sense can one personality ever "know" another? What relation do our various memories of a single object bear to the "real" object? What remains when a personality has been "spilt on air" and exists only as a group of contradictory impressions in others, who are also moving towards death? In what way does time condition human experience and its values? Out of that complex of retrospect and anticipation which is consciousness, what knowledge can emerge, what vision can be achieved? These are further problems which the book's form and content are designed to illuminate.

And so, with this limited collection of characters—the Ramsays and their guests—Virginia Woolf passes from one consciousness to another, from one group to another, exploring the significance of their reactions, following the course of their meditations, carefully arranging and patterning the images that rise up in their minds, bringing together, with care and economy, a select number of symbolic incidents, until a design has been achieved, the solidity of objective things breaks down, and experience is seen as something fluid though with definite shape, inexpressible yet significant.

In *Mrs. Dalloway* Virginia Woolf set the scene of her action with precision. We know at any given moment what part of London we are in. Streets and buildings are given their real names, and carefully particularized. But in *To the Lighthouse* for the first time in a full-length novel Virginia Woolf reduces the particularizing details of the setting to a minimum. We know, from one fleeting reference, that we are on an island in the Hebrides[1] but that is all the information we get. For the rest, we learn that the Ramsay's house is within walking distance of the "town" and situated on a bay. It is clear that Virginia Woolf is here more concerned with conveying a general impression of sea, sand and rocks than with describing any particular place. It is a symbolic setting: this group of people temporarily isolated from the rest of society on this remote island represents a microcosm of society, while the background of natural scenery provides images and suggestions that can be used as interpretative symbols. Throughout the book the characters are presented and represented until they are finally seen as symbolic. We are shown now their own minds, now their reactions on the minds of others, now the memory they leave when they are gone, now their relation to the landscape, till eventually all this adds up to something barely expressible (indeed not directly expressible at all) yet significant. For a split second everything falls into a pattern, and then the meaning is lost again, as (to employ a simile that keeps recurring in *To the Lighthouse*) we look out of the windows of a speeding train and see for one brief moment a group of figures that conveys some strange new meaning. With the temporary attainment of maximum pattern the book ends. Lily Bris-

---

[1] There are precisely three indications of the locality of the setting in *To the Lighthouse*. "Scotland" is mentioned on page 44 (Harcourt, Brace Edition): "and no lockmaker in the whole of Scotland can mend a bolt." A map of the Hebrides is referred to on page 170. And when Minta loses her brooch, Paul resolves that if he could not find it "he would slip out of the house at dawn when they were all asleep and if he could not find it he would go to Edinburgh and buy her another." Glasgow, however, and not Edinburgh would be the obvious city to go to if they were anywhere in the Hebrides, so this reference is misleading. The present writer, who knows the west coast of Scotland, has amused himself by trying to pin down the island, but has found that it is impossible to do so. The details given by Virginia Woolf are at once too general to be identified with any particular place and too specific (position of the beach, distance from the lighthouse, relation to "the town," type of vegetation, etc.) to be made to fit in with any spot chosen at random. What island in the Hebrides is there, large enough to contain a "town" (p. 18, etc.), yet small enough to appear "very small," "like a leaf," when one had sailed only a few miles away; possessing both cliffs, "park-like prospects," trees, sandy beaches, sand dunes (p. 105), accommodating at walking distance from the "town" a large house with lawn, cultivated garden, tennis court, and other amenities, and with local inhabitants named McNab (the charwoman) and Macalister (the boatman). Neither Macalister nor McNab is an Island name. Virginia Woolf's scene is either a composite one (with perhaps some suggestions from Cornwall) or largely imaginary.

coe, the painter, the spinster who will not marry and keeps looking
for the proper significance of characters and scenes, is deputy for the
author: when she, thinking of the now dead Mrs. Ramsay and of
Mr. Ramsay off in the boat to the lighthouse, and endeavouring at
the same time to find the proper way of finishing her picture, finally
has her "vision," the pattern is complete, she finishes her painting,
and the book ends. The Ramsays have at last landed at the lighthouse.
Lily Briscoe, thinking of them as she paints, recognizes their landing
as somehow significant. So does old Mr. Carmichael, who has been
dozing in a chair on the lawn not far from her. And the final threads
come together:

> "He has landed," she said aloud. "It is finished." Then, surging up,
> puffing slightly, old Mr. Carmichael stood beside her, looking like an old
> pagan god, shaggy, with weeds in his hair and the trident (it was only
> a French novel) in his hand. He stood by her on the edge of the lawn,
> swaying a little in his bulk, and said, shading his eyes with his hand:
> "They will have landed," and she felt that she had been right. They had
> not needed to speak. They had been thinking the same things and he
> had answered her without her asking him anything. He stood there as if
> he were spreading his hands over all the weakness and suffering of man-
> kind; she thought he was surveying, tolerantly and compassionately,
> their final destiny. Now he has crowned the occasion, she thought, when
> his hand slowly fell, as if she had seen him let fall from his great height
> a wreath of violets and asphodels which, fluttering slowly, lay at length
> upon the earth.
>
> Quickly, as if she were recalled by something over there, she turned to
> her canvas. There it was—her picture. Yes, with all its greens and blues,
> its lines running up and across, its attempt at something. It would be
> hung in the attics, she thought; it would be destroyed. But what did that
> matter? she asked herself, taking up her brush again. She looked at the
> steps; they were empty; she looked at her canvas; it was blurred. With a
> sudden intensity, as if she saw it clear for a second, she drew a line there,
> in the centre. It was done; it was finished. Yes, she thought, laying down
> her brush in extreme fatigue, I have had my vision.

The characters in *To the Lighthouse* are carefully arranged in
their relation to each other, so that a definite symbolic pattern
emerges. Mr. Ramsay, the professor of philosophy, who made one
original contribution to thought in his youth and has since been re-
peating and elaborating it without being able to see through to the
ultimate implications of his system; his wife, who knows more of
life in an unsystematic and intuitive way, who has no illusions ("There
was no treachery too base for the world to commit; she knew that. No
happiness lasted; she knew that.") yet presides over her family with a
calm and competent efficiency; Lily Briscoe, who refuses to get married and tries to express her sense of reality in terms of colour and

form; Charles Tansley, the aggressive young philosopher with an inferiority complex; old Mr. Carmichael, who dozes unsocially in the sun and eventually turns out to be a lyric poet; Minta Doyle and Paul Rayley, the undistinguished couple whom Mrs. Ramsay gently urges into a not too successful marriage—each character has a very precise function in this carefully organized story. The lighthouse itself, standing lonely in the midst of the sea, is a symbol of the individual who is at once a unique being and a part of the flux of history. To reach the lighthouse is, in a sense, to make contact with a truth outside oneself, to surrender the uniqueness of one's ego to an impersonal reality. Mr. Ramsay, who is an egotist constantly seeking applause and encouragement from others, resents his young son's enthusiasm for visiting the lighthouse, and only years later, when his wife has died and his own life is almost worn out, does he win this freedom from self—and it is significant that Virginia Woolf makes Mr. Ramsay escape from his egotistic preoccupations for the first time just before the boat finally reaches the lighthouse. Indeed, the personal grudges nourished by each of the characters fall away just as they arrive; Mr. Ramsay ceases to pose with his book and breaks out with an exclamation of admiration for James's steering; James and his sister Cam lose their resentment at their father's way of bullying them into this expedition and cease hugging their grievances: "What do you want? they both wanted to ask. They both wanted to say, Ask us anything and we will give it you. But he did not ask them anything." And at the moment when they land, Lily Briscoe and old Mr. Carmichael, who had not joined the expedition, suddenly develop a mood of tolerance and compassion for mankind, and Lily has the vision which enables her to complete her picture.

There is a colour symbolism running right through the book. When Lily Briscoe is wrestling unsuccessfully with her painting, in the first part of the book, she sees the colours as "bright violet and staring white," but just as she achieves her final vision at the book's conclusion, and is thus able to complete her picture, she notices that the lighthouse "had melted away into a blue haze"; and though she sees the canvas clearly for a second before drawing the final line, the implication remains that this blurring of colours is bound up with her vision. Mr. Ramsay, who visualizes the last, unattainable, step in his philosophy as glimmering *red* in the distance, is contrasted with the less egotistical Lily, who works with blues and greens, and with Mrs. Ramsay, who is indicated on Lily's canvas as "a triangular purple shape." Red and brown appear to be the colours of individuality and egotism, while blue and green are the colours of impersonality. Mr. Ramsay, until the very end of the book, is represented as an egotist, and his colour is red or brown; Lily is the impersonal artist, and her colour is blue; Mrs. Ramsay stands somewhere between, and her colour is purple.[2] The journey to the lighthouse is the journey from egotism to impersonality.

But it is much more than that. The story opens with Mrs. Ramsay promising young James that if it is fine they will go to the lighthouse tomorrow, whereupon Mr. Ramsay points out that it won't be fine, and arouses James's long lived resentment. It concludes, ten years later when Mrs. Ramsay is dead and James is sixteen, with the arrival of Mr. Ramsay, James and Cam at the lighthouse and the shedding at that moment of all their personal grudges and resentments—all of which synchronize with Lily's achievement of her vision. The story is obviously more than the contrast between the initial and the final situation, for between these two points there is an abundance of detail —description of character and of characters' thought processes—and a number of symbolic situations which widen the implications of the book as it proceeds and prevents the reader from identifying its meaning with any single "moral."

The theme of the relation of the individual to existence as a whole is treated in a variety of ways. It recurs as a constantly shifting thought pattern in character after character. Lily Briscoe, the artist, is observing Mr. Ramsay, philosopher and egotist:

> Lily Briscoe went on putting away her brushes, looking up, looking down. Looking up, there he was—Mr. Ramsay—advancing towards them, swinging, careless, oblivious, remote. A bit of a hypocrite? she

[2] There is a beautiful example of this colour symbolism on p. 270 (Harcourt, Brace Edition): "Wherever she happened to be, painting, here, in the country or in London, the vision would come to her, and her eyes, half closing, sought something to base her vision on. She looked down the railway carriage, the omnibus; took a line from shoulder or cheek; looked at the windows opposite; at Piccadilly, lamp-strung in the evening. All had been part of the fields of death. But always something —it might be a face, a voice, a paper boy crying *Standard, News*—thrust through, snubbed her, waked her, required and got in the end an effort of attention, so that the vision must be perpetually remade. Now again, moved as she was by some instinctive need of distance and blue, she looked at the bay beneath her, making hillocks of the blue bars of the waves, and stony fields of the purpler spaces, again she was roused as usual by something incongruous. There was a brown spot in the middle of the bay. It was a boat. Yes, she realised that after a second. But whose boat? Mr. Ramsay's boat, she replied. Mr. Ramsay; the man who had marched past her, with his hand raised, aloof, at the head of a procession, in his beautiful boots, asking her for sympathy, which she had refused. The boat was now half way across the bay." This passage, while taking its place naturally in the development of the story, at the same time throws an important light on the earlier and later parts of the book, clarifying symbolism and enriching significance. The artist, having an "instinctive need of . . . blue," sees Mr. Ramsay's boat as a *brown* spot on a *blue* sea. Brown is the personal colour, the egotistic colour; blue belongs to the impersonality of the artist.

repeated. Oh, no—the most sincere of men, the truest (here he was), the best; but, looking down, she thought, he is absorbed in himself, he is tyrannical, he is unjust; and kept looking down, purposely, for only so could she keep steady, staying with the Ramsays. Directly one looked up and saw them, what she called "being in love" flooded them. They became part of that unreal but penetrating and exciting universe which is the world seen through the eyes of love. The sky stuck to them; the birds sang through them. And, what was even more exciting, she felt, too, as she saw Mr. Ramsay bearing down and retreating, and Mrs. Ramsay sitting with James in the window and the cloud moving and the tree bending, how life, from being made up of little separate incidents which one lived one by one, became curled and whole like a wave which bore one up with it and threw one down with it, there, with a dash on the beach.

Speculations of this kind are constantly juxtaposed to specific incidents, which take on a symbolic quality in the light of the juxtaposition:

Standing now, apparently transfixed, by the pear tree, impressions poured in upon her of those two men, and to follow her thought was like following a voice which speaks too quickly to be taken down by one's pencil, and the voice was her own voice saying without prompting undeniable, everlasting, contradictory things, so that even the fissures and humps on the bark of the pear tree were irrevocably fixed there for eternity. You have greatness, she continued, but Mr. Ramsay has none of it. He is petty, selfish, vain, egotistical; he is spoilt; he is a tyrant; he wears Mrs. Ramsay to death; but he has what you (she addressed Mr. Bankes) have not; a fiery unworldliness; he knows nothing about trifles; he loves dogs and his children. He has eight. Mr. Bankes has none. Did he not come down in two coats the other night and let Mrs. Ramsay trim his hair into a pudding basin? All of this danced up and down, like a company of gnats, each separate, but all marvellously controlled in an invisible elastic net—danced up and down in Lily's mind, in and about the branches of the pear tree, where still hung in effigy the scrubbed kitchen table, symbol of her profound respect for Mr. Ramsay's mind, until her thought which had spun quicker and quicker exploded of its own intensity; she felt released; a shot went off close at hand, and there came, flying from its fragments, frightened, effusive, tumultuous, a flock of starlings.

"Jasper!" said Mr. Bankes. They turned the way the starlings flew, over the terrace. Following the scatter of swift-flying birds in the sky they stepped through the gap in the high hedge straight into Mr. Ramsay, who boomed tragically at them, "Some one had blundered!"

The stream of consciousness of one character enables us to see individual actions of other characters in their proper symbolic meaning. It is a subtle and effective device.

It would take too much space to discuss the minor devices employed by Virginia Woolf in order to help expand the meaning into something profounder yet vaguer than any specific thesis. The main theme concerns the relation of personality, death, and time to each other; the relation of the individual to the sum of experience in general. Many devices are used to suggest this problem—presented less as a problem than as a situation, a quality in life on which the significance of living depends. Minor points such as the characteristic gesture of Mr. Ramsay (raising his hand as if to avert something), symbolic images such as the hand cleaving the blue sea, specific ideas suggested in the thought process of one or other of the characters (each of whom can be made at any time to speak for the author by any one of a number of devices which present that character as having momentarily transcended the limitations of his personality and glimpsed some kind of eternal truth)—all help to enrich the implications of the story. Here, for example, is Lily Briscoe, symbol of the artist and his relation to experience:

> She wanted to go straight up to him and say, "Mr. Carmichael!" Then he would look up benevolently as always, from his smoky vague green eyes. But one only woke people if one knew what one wanted to say to them. And she wanted to say not one thing, but everything. Little words that broke up the thought and dismembered it said nothing. "About life, about death; about Mrs. Ramsay"—no, she thought, one could say nothing to nobody. The urgency of the moment always missed its mark. Words fluttered sideways and struck the object inches too low. Then one gave it up; then the idea sunk back again; then one became like most middle-aged people, cautious, furtive, with wrinkles between the eyes and a look of perpetual apprehension. For how could one express in words these emotions of the body? express that emptiness there? (She was looking at the drawing-room steps; they looked extraordinarily empty.) It was one's body feeling, not one's mind. The physical sensations that went with the bare look of the steps had become suddenly extremely unpleasant. . . . Oh, Mrs. Ramsay! she called out silently, to that essence which sat by the boat, that abstract one made of her, that woman in grey, as if to abuse her for having gone, and then having gone, come back again. It had seemed so safe, thinking of her. Ghost, air, nothingness, a thing you could play with easily and safely at any time of day or night, she had been that, and then suddenly she put her hand out and wrung the heart thus. . . .
>
> "What does it mean? How do you explain it all?" she wanted to say, turning to Mr. Carmichael again. For the whole world seemed to have dissolved in this early morning hour into a pool of thought, a deep basin of reality, and one could almost fancy that had Mr. Carmichael spoken, for instance, a little tear would have rent the surface pool. And then? Something would emerge. A hand would be shoved up, a blade would be flashed. It was nonsense of course.

Here the thoughts and images contained in a character's reverie
reflect back and forth on other aspects of the story and enrich the
meaning of the whole.

Finally, the reader might ponder on the symbolism of the window
in the first section. Mr. Ramsay paces up and down in the growing
darkness outside, while Mrs. Ramsay and James sit by the window,
watching him pass back and forth. There is a detailed symbolism here,
as deliberate, though not so obvious, as that of Maeterlinck's *Interior*.

Virginia Woolf's characteristic concern with the relation of personality to time, change and death is manifested in her treatment of the
character of Mrs. Ramsay, who is alive in the first section and whose
death is recorded parenthetically in the "Time Passes" interlude. Yet
her personality dominates the book: she lives, in section three, in the
memory of the others; her character has become part of history, including and determining the present. As she is about to finish her
painting Lily Briscoe thinks of Mrs. Ramsay as still influential after
death:

> Mrs. Ramsay, she thought, stepping back and screwing up her eyes. (It
> must have altered the design a good deal when she was sitting on the
> step with James. There must have been a shadow.) When she thought
> of herself and Charles throwing ducks and drakes and of the whole
> scene on the beach, it seemed to depend somehow upon Mrs. Ramsay
> sitting under the rock, with a pad on her knee, writing letters. (She wrote
> innumerable letters, and sometimes the wind took them and she and
> Charles just saved a page from the sea.) But what a power was in the
> human soul! she thought. That woman sitting there writing under the
> rock resolved everything into simplicity; made these angers, irritations
> fall off like old rags; she brought together this and that and then
> this, and so made out of that miserable silliness and spite (she and
> Charles squabbling, sparring, had been silly and spiteful) something—
> this scene on the beach for example, this moment of friendship and
> liking—which survived, after all these years complete, so that she dipped
> into it to re-fashion her memory of him, and there it stayed in the mind
> affecting one almost like a work of art.

And she goes on to speculate on the present significance of the
woman who had been dead now for five years:

> What is the meaning of life? That was all—a simple question; one that
> tended to close in on one with years. The great revelation had never
> come. The great revelation perhaps never did come. Instead there were
> little daily miracles, illuminations, matches struck unexpectedly in the
> dark; here was one. This, that, and the other; herself and Charles
> Tansley and the breaking wave; Mrs. Ramsay bringing them together;
> Mrs. Ramsay saying, "Life stand still here"; Mrs. Ramsay making of

the moment something permanent (as in another sphere Lily herself tried to make of the moment something permanent)—this was of the nature of a revelation. In the midst of chaos there was shape; this eternal passing and flowing (she looked at the clouds going and the leaves shaking) was struck into stability. Life stand still here, Mrs. Ramsay said. "Mrs. Ramsay! Mrs. Ramsay!" she repeated. She owed it all to her.

One can compare this with the reverie of Mrs. Dalloway on learning of the death of Septimus Warren Smith; the way of relating one character to another is not dissimilar. And just as, at the end of the former book, Mrs. Dalloway suddenly has her final illumination after she has watched the old woman opposite go into her bedroom and pull down the blind, so Lily, sitting painting outside the Ramsay's house, sees, just before her final vision, somebody come into the room behind the window:

> Suddenly the window at which she was looking was whitened by some light stuff behind it. At last then somebody had come into the drawing-room; somebody was sitting in the chair. For Heaven's sake, she prayed, let them sit still there and not come floundering out to talk to her. Mercifully, whoever it was stayed still inside; had settled by some stroke of luck so as to throw an odd-shaped triangular shadow over the step. It altered the composition of the picture a little. It was interesting. It might be useful. Her mood was coming back to her. One must keep on looking without for a second relaxing the intensity of emotion, the determination not to be put off, not to be bamboozled. One must hold the scene—so—in a vise and let nothing come in and spoil it. One wanted, she thought, dipping her brush deliberately, to be on a level with ordinary experience, to feel simply that's a chair, that's a table, and yet at the same time, It's a miracle, it's an ecstasy. The problem might be solved after all. Ah, but what had happened? Some wave of white went over the window pane. The air must have stirred some flounce in the room. Her heart leapt at her and seized her and tortured her.
>
> "Mrs. Ramsay! Mrs. Ramsay!" she cried, feeling the old horror come back—to want and want and not to have. Could she inflict that still? And then, quietly, as if she refrained, that too became part of ordinary experience, was on a level with the chair, with the table. Mrs. Ramsay —it was part of her perfect goodness—sat there quite simply, in the chair, flicked her needles to and fro, knitted her reddish-brown stocking, cast her shadow on the step. There she sat.

Symbolically, the past returns and shapes the present. Mrs. Ramsay comes back into Lily Briscoe's picture, as she had been part of the original design ten years before, and out of this meeting of two very different personalities across the years the final insight results. Across the water at the same moment Mr. Ramsay, by his praise of James's handling of the boat, is exorcising the ghost of James's early resentment, also ten years old, and all the threads of the story are finally coming together. It is a masterly piece of construction.

To the Lighthouse is a work in which plot, locale, and treatment are so carefully bound up with each other that the resulting whole is more finely organized and more effective than anything else Virginia Woolf wrote. The setting in an indefinite island off the northwest coast of Scotland enables her to indulge in her characteristic symbolic rarifications with maximum effect, for here form and content fit perfectly and inevitably. Middle-class London is not, perhaps, the best scene for a tenuous meditative work of this kind, and *Mrs. Dalloway* might be said to suffer from a certain incompatibility between the content and the method of treatment. A misty island is more effective than a London dinner party as the setting for a novel of indirect philosophic suggestion, and as a result qualities of Virginia Woolf's writing which in her other works tend to appear if not as faults at least as of doubtful appropriateness, are seen in this work to their fullest advantage. In *To the Lighthouse* Virginia Woolf found a subject that enabled her to do full justice to her technique.

Virginia's Web

by Geoffrey H. Hartman

This goddess of the continuum is incapable of continuity.
Valéry, on the Pythoness

Transitions may well be the hardest part of a writer's craft: Virginia Woolf shows they are also the most imaginative. One remembers, from *Mrs. Dalloway*, the inscrutable motor-car proceeding toward Piccadilly, and the way it serves to move the plot with it. Or, in the next episode, how the sky-writing plane moves different minds, each guessing at the slogan being dispensed, and then dispersed. The wind stealing the smoky letters before any guess is confirmed is the same that, fifteen years later, miscarries the players' words in *Between the Acts*. Suppose now that these letters or words or glimpses are divided by years, by some indefinite or immeasurable gap. We know that years pass, that words are spoken or spelt, and that cars reach their destination: yet the mystery lies in space itself, which the imaginative mind must fill, perhaps too quickly. The dominant issues in the study of Virginia Woolf have been her solipsism and her treatment of time and character; I propose to suspend them, and to see her novels as mirrors held up primarily to the imagination.

Let us consider a fairly simple passage from *To the Lighthouse*. To look at it closely needs a concern, a prior interest: in our case, how the novelist goes from one thing to another. The context of the passage is as follows. Mr. Ramsay and his two children, Cam and James, are being ferried to the Lighthouse. The weather is calm, and it seems the boat will never get there; Cam and James, moreover, do not want it to get there, resenting the tyrannous will of their father. In the first section of the novel, with Mrs. Ramsay still alive, it is he who damps the childish eagerness of James to go to the Lighthouse;

"Virginia's Web" by Geoffrey H. Hartman. From Chicago Review *14, no. 4 (Spring 1961): 20–32. Copyright © 1970 by Geoffrey H. Hartman. Reprinted by permission of the author.*

and now (many years later) he insists on this outing as a commemorative act:

> The sails flapped over their heads. The water chuckled and slapped the sides of the boat, which drowsed motionless in the sun. Now and then the sails rippled with a little breeze in them, but the ripple ran over them and ceased. The boat made no motion at all. Mr. Ramsay sat in the middle of the boat. He would be impatient in a moment, James thought, and Cam thought, looking at her father who sat in the middle of the boat between them (James steered; Cam sat alone in the bow) with his legs tightly curled. He hated hanging about.

The continuity is kept on the verbal as well as visual plane by echo and repetition (flapped, slapped, drowsed, them, them, boat, boat). This is an intensifying device any writer might use, but one is hardly aware with what skill the sentences lead inward, to that parenthesis and fine slowing-up that encompasses boat, man, and children. Mrs. Woolf's style is here at its best, and the continuities going from the freest to the stillest part of the scene (from the sail to the middle of the boat) do this with an almost humorous resistance. It is interesting to think that the rhythm should be generated by an avoidance; there is, in any case, a "stop and go" pattern to it, magnified perhaps by the subject of the passage. In terms of plot or subject we have a pause, in terms of the prose that describes it a sustained if not augmented interest in continuity. As the description reaches the inside of the boat, and then the inside of the mind, the rhythm slows, and as the rhythm slows the continuity is made more obvious as if to counterpoint the pausing. This pattern, however, may be found elsewhere too, and cannot be purely an intensifying or descriptive device. It may originate in the writer prior to the particular subject.

I am suggesting that continuity is a deeper matter here than craft or style. In his first important essay Valéry remarked that the extension of continuity by means of metaphor, language, or other means, was the common gift of genius. His thesis implied two things: that there is "space" or apparent discontinuity, and that the genial inventor can project his mind into it. If we identify this ability to project (or better, interpolate) with imagination, then the crucial question is what this "space" may be. There can be only one answer which is not a gross generalization, and this is *anything*. We are dealing, it must be remembered, with appearances, and there is nothing that may not succumb to blankness.[1] Art respects appearances so much that every-

[1] For a strictly philosophical account, see Hegel's *Phenomenology of Mind*, the Introduction and opening section on "Sense-Certainty," Heidegger's *What is Metaphysics* (1929), and Sartre's *L'Imaginaire* (1940). The experience I talk of in this rough and cursory way is that of "Nothingness."

thing may become questionably blank, even the continuities firmly established by science. For though science has shown them to exist it has not shown why they should exist so unapparently, and the formula that proves them also proves the coyness of Nature.

To the Lighthouse begins with a sense of fulness and continuous life as we are led in and out of Mrs. Ramsay's mind. There are few apparent "pauses" to threaten the continuity of thought or existence. The dark space between the beams of the Lighthouse does, however, penetrate consciousness. "A shutter, like the leathern eyelid of a lizard, flickered over the intensity of his gaze and obscured the letter R. In that flash of darkness he heard people saying—he was a failure —that R was beyond him. He would never reach R. On to R once more. R——" Mr. Ramsay's intellectual ambitions are described, and there are other fine sequences of the same kind.

These darker intervals, rare in the first part, consolidate as the encroaching and live darkness of the second part, which traces the gradual abandonment of the Ramsay house, and its last minute rescue from oblivion. Then, in the last section of the novel, a horrid calm moves directly into the heart of the characters. The becalming of the boat is part of a larger sequence, in which all are involved with death, present as distance or the sea's calm or the absence of Mrs. Ramsay. Each person is compelled by a stilling glance, like the bridegroom by the Wedding Guest. They must suffer the suspense, endure the calm, and ultimately resist it—its intimations of peace and of a happy death of the will.

Resistance is the major theme of this novel. The lighthouse itself is a monitory object, warning off, centered in hostile elements. Mr. Ramsay, an enemy of the sea that becalms his boat, is a stronger resister than Mrs. Ramsay who lives toward the sea. Resistance is a matter of imagination which can either actively fill "space," or passively blend with it and die. Imagination could also die to itself and become pure will, as in the case of Mr. Ramsay, who wishes to cross the sea, or from Q to R, by force. He denies space and violates the privacy of others. Yet to keep imagination alive involves staying alive to space, to the horrid calms of Virginia Woolf's ocean.

The imagination itself neither acknowledges nor denies space: it lives in it and says to every question "Life, life, life," like Orlando's little bird or Blake's cricket.[2] Affirmation, not meaning is basic to it, and the problem of meaning cannot even be faced without considering the necessity or fatality of some primary affirmation. Religious belief is such a primary act, but a special form of it. The found-

---

[2] *Orlando*, chapter 6; *Auguries of Innocence:* "A Riddle or the Cricket's Cry/ Is to Doubt a fit Reply."

ing of a fictional world is such a primary act. Fiction reveals something without which the mind could not be, or could not think. The mind needs a world, a substantialized Yes.

Yet every great artist rebels against this, and today his rebellion is conventional. By beginning to question the necessity of fiction, i.e., the inherently affirmative structure of imagination, he joins the philosopher who seeks a truth greater than that arbitrary Yes. The more Henry James seeks the definitive word the more his mind shrinks from affirmation. It is, similarly, Mrs. Woolf's resistance, her continuous doubting of the continuity she is forced to posit, we are interested in. At the end of *To the Lighthouse*, Lily Briscoe's "It is finished," referring in turn to the reaching of the Lighthouse and to her picture, is deeply ironic. It recalls a sufferance greater than the object attained by this last term, by any term. Each artist resists his own vision.

This resistance, however, cannot take place except in the space of fiction, and requires the creation of a work of art which is its own implicit critique. The reason that an artist's critique cannot be discursive, or purely so, is that it still involves an affirmation—the new work of art. It is therefore quite proper to put our question in strictly literary terms: What kind of novel does Mrs. Woolf write? And how does it criticize its origin in the affirmative impulse?

II

I shall try to define Virginia Woolf's novel as the product of a certain kind of prose and a certain kind of plot. This dyad should justify itself as we proceed, but what I say is experimental and may lead to some undue generalizing. The reason for omitting "character" should also appear: there is only one fully developed character in Mrs. Woolf's novels, and that is the completely expressive or "androgynous" mind.

Her concern for the novel is linked everywhere with that for prose style. She often remarks that prose, unlike poetry, is still in its infancy, and her first experimental novel, *Mrs. Dalloway*, matures it via the peregrinations of a woman's mind. It may be said with some truth that the novel is, for Virginia Woolf, simply the best form of presenting a completely expressive prose.

A Room of One's Own (1928) illustrates in slow-motion how this mature prose came to be. Mrs. Woolf's "sociological essay" is about the future of fiction and woman's part in it. But we are not given a straight essay. She refuses to separate her thought from certain imaginary accidents of time and place, and writes something akin to the French *récit*. Her mind, porous to the world even during thought, devises a prose similar to that of *To the Lighthouse,* which makes continuities out of distractions. It is as if a woman's mind were linked at its origin, like the novel itself, to romance; and one is quite happy with this natural picaresque, the author walking us and the world along on the back of her prose.

Still, prose in a novel is different from prose in some other form. Its function can be determined only within a particular structure, and a novel or story requires some finite series of events necessary to produce suspense and move the reader toward the resolving point. This raises the question of the relation of plot and prose.

In the modern novel there are at least two significant ways of making prose subsume the suspense previously offered by plot. One is to structure it as highly as the verse of the 17th Century classical drama in France, so that even the simplest conversation becomes dramatic. Henry James' prose has affinities to this. The other is to have the plot coincide with the special perspective of a character. Faulkner and many others (including James) may use this method, which creates a kind of mystery story, the mystery being the mind itself. Mrs. Woolf's prose has some affinities here, but it is not made to issue from a mind limited or peculiar enough to make us suspect the darkness it circles.

The curious fact is that neither the prose not the plot of Mrs. Woolf's novels can explain the suspense we feel. Perhaps suspense is the wrong word, since we are not avid for what happens next but fascinated by how the something next will happen. To understand this let us take *Mrs. Dalloway.* Its plot is simple and realistic as is always the case with Virginia Woolf (*Orlando* is only an apparent exception). The suspense or fascination cannot come from that source. Nor does it come, in isolation, from the rich prose woven by Clarissa's mind, since the plot often parts from her to present other people or views, yet our attention does not flag at those points. But if Mrs. Woolf goes at will beyond Clarissa's consciousness it is on condition that some line of continuity be preserved. There are no jumps, no chapters; every transition is tied to what precedes or has been introduced. The first line of the novel, "Mrs. Dalloway said she would buy the flowers herself," presupposes some immediate prior fact already taken up in consciousness, and is emblematic of the artist's mood throughout the novel. Our fascination is involved with this will to continuity, this free prose working under such strict conditions.

The plot, however, does play an important role. Clarissa waiting to cross the street, then crossing, is part of the plot; her thoughts while doing so effect many finer transitions. A tension is thus produced between the realistic plot and the expressive prose: the latter tends to veil or absorb the former, and the former suggests a more natural continuity, one less dependent on the mind. We know that certain things happen in sequence, that a play will go on, that people fall in love or cross streets, that a day moves from dawn to dusk. The simpler continuity of the plot tempts the mind forward, as a relief from the "essential prose," or as a resting place in something solid.

This tension between two types of continuity also makes the mind realize the artificial or arbitrary character of both. It is moved to conceive the void they bridge. A void is there, like the pauses or thoughts of death in Mrs Dalloway. But the mind conceives it joyfully, rather than in terror, because of the constant opening up of new perspectives, and the realization through this of its connective power. The continuities we have labeled "plot" and "prose" are, moreover, not unrelated or without special value. I would now like to show that they stand to each other dialectically as major types of affirmation, the plot-line coinciding mostly with what we call Nature, and the prose-line intimating something precarious but also perhaps greater, the "Nature that exists in works of mighty Poets." To do so I return to *A Room of One's Own*, in which Mrs. Woolf (or her persona) is thinking about women writers and the last of her thought sequences suggests the structure of her novels in microcosm.

III

Mrs. Woolf looks from her window at a London waking for the day's business in the Fall of '28. She looks out, not in, allowing herself to be distracted. The city seems to be indifferent to her concerns, and she records the fact strongly: "Nobody, it seemed, was reading *Antony and Cleopatra* . . . Nobody cared a straw—and I do not blame them—for the future of fiction, the death of poetry or the development by the average woman of a prose style completely expressive of her mind. If opinions upon any of these matters had been chalked on the pavement, nobody would have stooped to read them . . . Here came an errand-boy; here a woman with a dog on a lead. . . ."[3]

Something is wrong. Can a writer be so calm about indifference, especially when it threatens art? But Mrs. Woolf was hastening the end. Not her own, but the end of a civilization which had exalted one part of the soul at the expense of the rest. The twenties are reaching their close; the first world-war is not forgotten; Proust, Bergson, and Freud have advertised human possessiveness and male

---

[3] The thought-sequence from which I quote in this section is found in the last chapter (6) of *A Room of One's Own*.

arbitrariness, the subtlest workings-out of the patriarchal will. The bustle she welcomes has, at least, the arbitrariness of life rather than of the will: an errand boy here, a funeral there, business men, idlers, shoppers, each going his own way.

But her thought does not stop at this point: she lets it found its dialectic. The mind, to begin with, accepts a life indifferent to itself. The affirmative movement is not overcome, though what V. Woolf affirms is life rather than her will. Yet she is less interested in life as such than in the life of the mind which can only appear if thought is left as apparently free as the goings and comings beneath her window.

That this freedom may be an illusion does not matter. It is still a window to the truth and, in any case, lasts a short time. Mrs. Woolf continuing to look, the life disappears and only the indifference remains: ". . . there was a complete lull and suspension of traffic. Nothing came down the street; nobody passed. A single leaf detached itself from the plane tree at the end of the street, and in that pause and suspension fell." Her mind, however, will not accept this pause, this emptiness. The affirmative movement attaches itself the more strongly to the slightest sign. "Somehow it was like a signal falling, a signal pointing to a force in things which one had overlooked."

What the mind has overlooked seems at first to be Nature, an impersonally and constantly active principle of life. This certainly has a presence in Mrs. Woolf's novels. It is much more important to her than the spice of illusionistic realism. In her wish for a purer affirmation, one which does not merely go *toward* the male will, she often has her characters go toward Nature. Their direct relationships are diverted by a second one, "human beings not always in their relation to each other but in their relation to reality; and the sky too, and the trees or whatever it may be in themselves." No human being, she adds, should shut out the view.

Yet it becomes clear, as Mrs. Woolf continues, that the mind had also overlooked something in itself. The falling leaf reminds her, it is true, of a natural force, but *in the artist.* It is the artist, the person at the window, who affirms a world where there is none. She imagines that the signal points to "a river, which flowed past, invisibly round the corner, down the street, and took people and eddied them along." In *Mrs. Dalloway* the author's consciousness is precisely this: a stream of prose that moves people together and apart, entering at will this mind and that. Nature, as she now conceives it, is one in which the artist participates, so that Shakespeare, poetry, and the finding of a new prose style become once again vital issues.

The artist, at this point, is clearly a Prospero figure. She stages an illusion whose object is a marriage: the mind coming together outside of itself by means of the world or the stage. Nature and Art conspire for this illusion or prothalamion; the river, we notice, is a natural and artificial image of *rhythm,* and leads directly to the closing event. As if the river had eddied them together, a girl in patent leather boots and a young man in a maroon raincoat meet a taxi beneath Virginia Woolf's window and get in. "The sight was ordinary enough," she remarks, "what was strange was the rhythmical order with which my imagination had invested it."

Only now does she withdraw from the window, reflecting on the mind. Because of her topic—the woman as writer—she had been thinking intensely of one sex as distinct from the other. But, seeing the couple, the mind felt as if after being divided it had come together again in a natural fusion. Perhaps, she goes on, a state of mind exists in which one could continue without effort, because nothing is required to be repressed, and no resistance develops. Interpreting the event literally as well as analogically, she concludes that the fully functioning mind is androgynous.

There is much fantasy in this. What remains is a sustained act of thought, a dialectic that comprises certain distinct types of affirmation. "Dialectic" is not, at first glance, the right word, since all we see is an affirmative movement increasing in scope. There comes, however, a critical pause, a moment of discontinuity, in which the *negative* almost appears. "Nothing came down the street; nobody passed." Such "power failures" are not rare in Virginia Woolf, and not always so lightly overcome. They assume a cosmic proportion in her last novel. Miss La Trobe, the illusionist, cannot sustain her country pageant. The wind is against her, life is against her, the rhythm breaks. She learns the depth of space between her and her creation; the vacuum, also, between it and the audience. "Miss La Trobe leant against the tree, paralyzed. Her power had left her. Beads of perspiration broke on her forehead. Illusion had failed. 'This is death,' she murmured, 'death.'" At this very moment, as in the scene beneath Virginia Woolf's window, Nature seems to take over and reestablish the rhythm in an expressionistic passage revealing the complicity of Art and Nature: "Then, suddenly, as the illusion petered out, the cows took up the burden. One had lost her calf. In the very nick of time she lifted her great moon-eyed head and bellowed. All the great moon-eyed heads laid themselves back. From cow after cow came the same yearning bellow. . . . The cows annihilated the gap; bridged the distance; filled the emptiness and continued the emotion."

Between the Acts reveals the same voracious desire for continuity as *Mrs. Dalloway* and *To the Lighthouse,* yet in this last work the novelist has dropped all pretense as to the realism of her transitions. She is outrageously, sadly humorous. "Suddenly the cows

stopped; lowered their heads, and began browsing. Simultaneously
the audience lowered their heads and read their programmes." This
is how she gets from the cows to the audience, with the result, of
course, that one feels the space she bridges more intensely. Yet does
not the whole novel turn on what is *between* the acts, on the interpolations of the novelist who continually saves the play for Miss La
Trobe? As in the example from *A Room of One's Own*, it is finally
irrelevant whether the continuities discovered by V. Woolf are in
Nature or in the Artist.

Our question as to the kind of novel Virginia Woolf writes can
now be answered. There is a line of development which goes from
the "realism" of *The Voyage Out* (1915) to the "expressionism" of
Between the Acts (1941), and passes through the experimental period
of 1925–31, containing *Mrs. Dalloway, To the Lighthouse, Orlando,*
and *The Waves.*[4] Mrs. Woolf sought to catch the power of affirmation in its full extent, and her effort to do so includes this shuttling
between realistic and expressionistic forms of style. She never abandoned realism entirely because it corresponds to an early phase of
affirmation. It is realism of the simple and illusionistic kind which
guides our powers of belief toward the world we see, when we see it
most freely. We can call this world Nature, understanding by that
a continuous yet relatively impersonal principle of life, even when
(as in the bustle beneath Virginia Woolf's window) it assumes a more
human shape. The next phase, more complex, raises the problem of
"interpolation." The falling leaf is a signal from Nature, but it points
to the artist who sees or affirms a Nature persisting through the negative moment. Art, therefore, becomes interpolation, rather than
mimesis. Though Mrs. Woolf retains a realistic plot, everything of
importance tends to happen between the acts, between each finite
or external sign. *Mrs. Dalloway* and *To the Lighthouse* are distinguished by this indefinite expansion of the interval, of the mind-
space, for example, between the beams of the Lighthouse. The
realistic plot is sustained by an expressionistic continuity.

Let us provisionally omit *The Waves* and go to Virginia Woolf's
last novel. Though its plot is as realistic as ever, we cannot any longer
tell with complete certainty what *really* happens between the acts

---

[4] I am probably unfair in omitting *Jacob's Room* (1922) from the experimental
novels. The link between imagination and interpolation is gropingly acknowledged:
"But something is always impelling one to hum vibrating, like the hawk moth, at
the mouth of the cavern of mystery, endowing Jacob Flanders with all sorts of
qualities he had not at all—for though, certainly, he sat talking to Bonamy, half
of what he said was too dull to repeat; much unintelligible (about unknown people
and Parliament); what remains is mostly a matter of guesswork. Yet over him we
hang vibrating."

that make up the action. The novel has a movement like that of Zeno's arrow: we know it flies continuously, and will reach some end, yet are still amazed it does not break in mid-flight. The author, another La Trobe, might fail the continuity, and history, the subject of the play, might fail likewise and not reach the present moment. But life and the novel continue in the same country manner because the artist's interpolations are imaginative enough.

In the case of *The Waves* we cannot even tell what happens. It is not that the plot-line is unclear, but now everything is interpolation, even the characters who are simply their speeches, and these speeches interpret acts that might and might not have been. What happens is what the speeches make happen. The purple prefaces alone, describing a day from dark to dark, seem to be founded in reality, or rather Nature: the human parts are pushed between as a supreme interpolation standing against the impersonal roll of time.

IV

Considered as notes toward a supreme fiction the novels of Virginia Woolf say "It must be affirmative." They suppose a mind with an immense, even unlimited power to see or build continuities. It is almost as if the special attribute of the Unconscious, that it does not know the negative, belonged also to Mind in its freest state. The artist is either not conscious of the negative (i.e. his Unconscious speaks through him) or *fiction* is generically the embodiment of the negative—and whatever dialectic characterizes Mind—in purely affirmative terms. The reader, of course, may reconstitute the negative; this task is one of the principal aims of interpretation. We have done a similar thing by pointing to the precarious and interpolative character of Virginia Woolf's continuities. In parts of *To the Lighthouse,* in the last chapter of *Orlando,* and in *The Waves,* the novel is brought to the limit of its capacity to show death, decay, repression, discontinuity . . . in terms of thought and speech and prose-rhythm. Irony is no longer a device; Art becomes irony and the reader sees that the extreme eloquence of *The Waves* hides silence and incommunicability, or that Mrs. Ramsay thinking to affirm life really affirms death.

I wish to make this irony more cogent by a last glance at Mrs. Ramsay. The first section of *To the Lighthouse* is called "The Window." Mrs. Ramsay (like her creator in *A Room of One's Own*) sits near a window, and knits. Her hands knit—so does her mind. Every strain that comes from without is absorbed by the regularity of her hands and the continuity of her mind. The strains are endless; she is besieged by eight children, by memory, by Nature, and above all

by a husband who constantly if surreptitiously demands her attention. Yet, as if another Penelope, apart from the clamoring suitors,
she sits and weaves an interminable garment.

Is it a dress or a shroud? A reddish brown stocking, of course, in
expectation of visiting the Lighthouse Keeper and his son, though
we will not see her arrive. She dies suddenly one night, and her
death reveals what she has woven. Darkness and decay creep over the
house which even now is none too tidy. Mrs Ramsay alive keeps the
disorder vital, and prevents it from overrunning. She is the natural
center, the sun, and however confused relationships get, it all comes
back to her, is resolved into simplicity by her word or presence. But
when she dies, impersonality, waste and vagueness flood the house like
a delayed judgment.

The second part of the novel, "Time Passes," describes the near-
ruin of the House of Ramsay. It reverts to the sea, to Nature; and the
human events breaking that slope are reported parenthetically, as
interpolations. The structure of *The Waves* comes directly out of
this second part. What can the author be saying but that there existed
a strange (perhaps not avoidable) correspondence between the mind
of Mrs. Ramsay and the will of Nature? Although most open to life,
sitting by the window, knitting every impulse into a fabric of thought
and feeling, what she worked proved finally to be a shroud. But
the male will survives in the form of Mr. Ramsay, a sparse, old, dom-
ineering man, still feeding on the sympathy of others.

It is, therefore, a tragic choice which confronts us. Mrs. Ramsay
is the feminine part of the soul, with its will to bypass the will, its
desire to let things be and grow in their own time, and above all with
its frightening power for mystical marriage, that refusal to sustain the
separateness of things in an overgreat anticipation of final unity.
This last is her profoundest trait (she is also literally a match-maker)
and it reveals her identification with death:

> Not as oneself did one find rest ever, in her experience (she accomplished
> here something dexterous with her needles) but as a wedge of darkness.
> Losing personality, one lost the fret, the hurry, the stir; and there rose
> to her lips always some exclamation of triumph over life when things
> came together in this peace, this rest, this eternity; and pausing there she
> looked out to meet that stroke of the Lighthouse, the long steady stroke,
> the last of the three, which was her stroke, for watching them in this
> mood always at this hour one could not help attaching oneself to one
> thing, especially of the things one saw; and this thing, the long steady
> stroke, was her stroke. Often she found herself sitting and looking, sit-
> ting and looking, with her work in her hands until she became the thing
> she looked at—that light for example. And it would lift up on it some
> little phrase or other which had been lying in her mind like that—
> "Children don't forget, children don't forget"—which she would

repeat and begin adding to it. It will end, it will end, she said. It will come, it will come, when suddenly she added, We are in the hands of the Lord.

This is Mrs. Ramsay's mind knitting, and she knows she has gone too far, hypnotized by her own rhythm. It was not she who said, We are in the hands of the Lord. "She had been trapped into saying something she did not mean." It is curious how at this moment Mrs. Ramsey echoes a mood which breaks into Shakespeare's tragedies imminently before the end. Do we not hear Desdemona's "All's one" and Hamlet's "If it be now, 'tis not to come; if it be not to come, it will be now; if it be not now, yet it will come"?[5] Despite her great longing for privacy, she cannot but help the reconciliation of all things, plots to marry off Paul and Minta, William Bankes and Lily Briscoe, subdues her judgment, and always finally gives in to her husband, betraying her soul and others for the sake of peace.

V

Virginia Woolf's use of a realistic plot and an expressionistic continuity seems to me as deep a solution to the structural problems of prose fiction as that found in *Ulysses*. Though the form cannot be said to originate with her,[6] she gave it a conscious and personal perfection, and it remains a vital compromise with the demands of realism. She learnt, of course, a great deal from (and against) Joyce, and to mention her in that company is itself a judgment. Her weakness, bound up with her virtues, lies less in any formal conception than in her subject, which is almost too specialized for the novel. I suspect that it is her subject, not her form, which is "poetic"; for she deals always with a part of the mind closest to the affirmative impulse. We do not find in her great "scenes," passionate and fatal interviews with the characters restricted to and revolving about each other. For however complex her characters may be, they are caught up essentially in one problem, and are variations of the "separatist" or "unifier" type. The one lives by doubting, and the other by affirming, the illusion of a divine or childhood Nature. Poetry gives us this Nature more vividly than V. Woolf, but it is she who makes us aware of its daily necessity and deception. Our doubt or affirmation shows equally the presence of its counterpart, Death—an alienation from life within life itself.

[5] Similar echoes and rhythms weave through the thoughts of Mrs. Dalloway ("Fear no more the heat o' the sun . . .") and play an interesting part in *Between the Acts*.
[6] Henry James is probably the nearest influence: one would have to distinguish both his interpolative method and the interior monologue from Virginia Woolf's "exterior" monologue.

To the Lighthouse (1927)

by Jean Guiguet

One afternoon in Tavistock Square, even before *Mrs. Dalloway* had reached the public, Virginia Woolf thought out her fifth novel, *To the Lighthouse*.[1] It came to her, as most frequently happened, quite unexpectedly, with sudden urgency, between essays and sketches[2] whose brevity proved both restful and stimulating after the long labour of *Mrs. Dalloway*. On May 14, 1925, we find it mentioned for the first time in *A Writer's Diary,* with its principal characteristics:

> This is going to be fairly short; to have father's character done complete in it; and mother's; and St. Ives; and childhood; and all the usual things I try to put in—life, death, etc. But the centre is father's character, sitting in a boat, reciting We perished, each alone, while he crushes a dying mackerel.

Yet this was only a germ which must be allowed to develop, for she adds:

> However, I must refrain. I must write a few little stories first and let the *Lighthouse* simmer, adding to it between tea and dinner till it is complete for writing out.[3]

Sketchy as this project is, it includes two points that are worth noting. On the one hand, the importance given to her characters as characters, if not in the traditional sense, at least in the sense implied in *Mrs. Dalloway;* which leads one, from the start, to expect similarity of treatment with the book's predecessor.

On the other hand, the theme of loneliness in death: its importance

---

"To the Lighthouse (*1927*)." *From* Virginia Woolf and Her Works *by Jean Guiguet, trans. by Jean Stewart (New York: Harcourt, Brace & World, Inc., 1965, London: The Hogarth Press, Ltd.), pp. 248–60. Copyright © 1962 by Jean Guiguet; translation © 1965 by The Hogarth Press. Reprinted by permission of the publishers.*

[1] Cf. AWD [*A Writer's Diary*] p. 106 (105): ". . . so I made up the *Lighthouse* one afternoon in the Square here."

[2] Cf. AWD p. 74 (73): Monday April 20 (1925): "I have now at least 6 stories welling up in me. . . ."

[3] AWD pp. 76–7 (75).

is emphasized by its association with the central figure; resuming one of the obsessions that haunt *Mrs. Dalloway*,[4] it promises an analogy of substance which combined with the analogy of form, will make this novel the natural sequel to the one she has just completed.

A month later, on June 14th, the broad lines of the novel are already laid down, somewhat too precisely perhaps for the author's liking,[5] since she dreads being confined within too narrow a framework which would not allow her latitude for the enrichments and excrescences which constitute the life of writing.[6] Between the superficial, bread-and-butter commitments of criticism consequent on the success of *The Common Reader,* the book takes shape in the depth of her mind,[7] surfacing indiscreetly at times to distract her from her writing.[8] The themes of death, solitude and memory intermingled, the sound of the sea in the background,[9] seem to steep these preliminary meditations in a very special colour, which impregnates the form in anticipation to such a point that Virginia Woolf realises the inadequacy of the word "novel" and seeks another to describe her work: "A new ——— by Virginia Woolf. But what? Elegy?" [10] This sense of overflowing the limits of the genre is here explicitly expressed for the first time: it grew constantly more marked until the end of her career.[11] By July, a fortnight before leaving for Rodmell, where she hoped to begin her book and complete it during her two months' stay, the project has ripened[12]; the division into three parts is settled: ". . . father and mother and child in the garden; the death; the sail to the Lighthouse." [13] Among possible enrichments, those she already envisages are, first, a number of compressed character

[4] Cf. *Mrs. Dalloway,* p. 103 (140): "Besides, now that he was quite alone, condemned, deserted, as those who are about to die are alone, there was a luxury in it, an isolation full of sublimity . . . ," and p. 202 (280–1): "Death was defiance. Death was an attempt to communicate, people feeling the impossibility of reaching the centre which, mystically, evaded them; closeness drew apart; rapture faded, one was alone. There was an embrace in death."

[5] Cf. AWD p. 78 (77): ". . . [I] have thought out, perhaps too clearly, *To the Lighthouse.*"

[6] Cf. AWD p. 80 (79): "I think, though, that when I begin it I shall enrich it in all sorts of ways, thicken it; give it branches—roots which I do not perceive now."

[7] Cf. AWD p. 80 (78): ". . . slipping tranquilly off into the deep water of my own thoughts navigating the underworld. . . ."

[8] Cf. AWD p. 80 (78): "But while I try to write, I am making up *To the Lighthouse.*"

[9] Cf. AWD p. 80 (78): ". . . the sea is to be heard all through it."

[10] Cf. AWD p. 80 (78).

[11] Cf. *infra,* p. 328.

[12] Cf. AWD p. 80 (79): ". . . having a superstitious wish to begin *To the Lighthouse* the first day at Monk's House. I now think I shall finish it in the two months there."

[13] AWD p. 80 (79).

sketches, then the world of childhood.[14] Meanwhile, however, two problems preoccupy her. The first is the fear of lapsing into the sentimentality which the subject, compact of intimate memories, invites irresistibly.[15] This apprehension is no doubt a highly personal one, the artist's reaction to the natural inclination of her sensibility— and also the origin of its antidote, her humour. But at the same time it is an echo of *Mrs. Dalloway,* the discrimination between sensibility and sentimentality being one of the problems raised by the personality of Clarissa.[16]

For the moment she thinks of resorting to a classic remedy, catharsis; and she considers getting rid of this dangerous propensity by giving vent to it freely in a story.[17] The second problem is a positive one: it concerns "this impersonal thing, which I'm dared to do by my friends, the flight of time and the consequent break of unity in my design." [18] This idea involves not only the second chapter— "seven years passed" at the time, "Time passes" in the final version— but the whole structure of the novel: it was the basic problem corresponding to that which she had solved for *Mrs. Dalloway* by her discovery of the "tunnelling process." The interest she takes in it reveals her determination to experiment and improve: "A new problem like that breaks fresh ground in one's mind; prevents the regular ruts." [19]

However, once at Rodmell, an attack of depression[20] not only renders her incapable of any steady work during the two months that were to have been devoted to *To the Lighthouse,* but confuses her ideas, undermines her powers of decision and raises doubts on the essential features of the book.[21] In point of fact, being deprived of her zest and energy, she realizes the danger of facile repetition: either

[14] Cf. AWD p. 80 (79): "It might contain all characters boiled down; and childhood. . . ."

[15] Cf. *infra,* note 244.

[16] Cf. Mrs D p. 41 (53–4): "She owed him words: 'sentimental,' 'civilised'; they started up every day of her life as if he guarded her. A book was sentimental. . . . 'Sentimental,' perhaps she was to be thinking of the past." And p. 210 (292): was "Clarissa pure-hearted; that was it. Peter would think her sentimental. So she was."

[17] Cf. AWD p. 80 (79): "The word 'sentimental' sticks in my gizzard (I'll write it out of me in a story . . .). But this theme may be sentimental. . . ." The anxiety was to persist until the book was in print, cf. AWD pp. 100 (98), 101 (100), 107 (106).

[18] AWD p. 80 (79).

[19] AWD pp. 80–1 (79).

[20] Cf. *supra,* ch. III, p. 85 ff.

[21] Cf. AWD p. 81 (79–80): "I am intolerably sleepy and annulled and so write here. I do want indeed to consider my next book, but I am inclined to wait for a clearer head. The thing is I vacillate between a single and intense character of father; and a far wider slower book. . . ."

a companion piece to *Mrs. Dalloway,* a novel dominated by a single character, or else a "far wider slower book" in which she would "run the risk of falling into the flatness of *N. & D.* [*Night and Day*]."[22]

A partial improvement in her health and a brilliant start toward the end of August were short-lived.[23] Not until February 1926[24] do we find her writing with ease and fluency, immersed, save for a brief period in the afternoons, in her novel, the whole of which is now present in her mind.[25] By April 29th she has finished the first part and started on the second,[26] her pace and enthusiasm no whit diminished by the abstract and unusual character of this section, which is completed on May 25th.[27] She expects to finish by the end of July. Difficulties arising over the last pages, time wasted on an essay about De Quincey,[28] and perhaps also too fine and too busy a summer,[29] postpone the completion date to September 13th.

Having completed this task with considerably less effort than *Jacob's Room* and *Mrs. Dalloway,*[30] she expresses her usual feelings of "relief and disappointment."[31] However, the revision and retyping —three times over for certain passages—which took from October 25, 1926, to January 14, 1927,[32] left her fairly satisfied. She writes that "it is easily the best of my books: fuller than *J's. R.* [*Jacob's Room*] and less spasmodic, occupied with more interesting things than *Mrs. D. . . .* It is freer and subtler, I think."[33] A second reading, shortly

[22] Cf. AWD p. 81 (80).

[23] Cf. AWD p. 82 (80): "I have made a very quick and flourishing attack on *To the Lighthouse. . . .*"

[24] Cf. AWD p. 85 (84), Feb. 23rd: "I am blown like an old flag by my novel." She must actually have started in early January 1926, since, expecting to finish it by the end of July, she allows seven months: cf. AWD p. 89 (88).

[25] Cf. AWD p. 85 (84): "I live entirely in it, and come to the surface rather obscurely . . . Of course it is largely known to me. . . ."

[26] Cf. AWD p. 88 (87): "Yesterday I finished the first part of *To the Lighthouse,* and today began the second."

[27] Cf. AWD p. 89 (88): "I have finished—sketchily I admit—the second part of *To the Lighthouse*—and may, then, have it all written over by the end of July."

[28] Cf. AWD p. 100 (99): "I am exacerbated by the fact that I spent four days last week hammering out de Quincey, which has been lying about since June. . . ."

[29] Cf. AWD p. 99 (97): "For the rest, Charleston, Tilton, *To the Lighthouse,* Vita, expeditions . . . such an August not come my way for years; bicycling; no settled work done, but advantage taken of air for going to the river or over the downs."

[30] Cf. AWD p. 85 (84): ". . . after that battle *Jacob's Room,* that agony—all agony but the end—*Mrs Dalloway,* I am now writing as fast and freely as I have written in the whole of my life. . . ." And p. 89 (88): "Compare this dashing fluency with *Mrs Dalloway* (save the end).

[31] Cf. AWD p. 100 (99).

[32] Cf. AWD p. 103 (102): "Since October 25th I have been revising and retyping (some parts three times over) and no doubt I should work at it again; but I cannot."

[33] AWD p. 102 (101).

before publication,[34] confirms this judgment, which is scarcely shaken by some friends' criticism[35] or the coolness of a review,[36] amply made up for by the book's success with the public and the enthusiasm of her own circle.[37]

The lighthouse that shines out at night, in the offing from the island where the Ramsays are spending their holidays with a group of friends, is the vanishing point, both material and symbolic, towards which all the lines of *To the Lighthouse* converge. James Ramsay, six years old, cutting out an old catalogue as he sits at the feet of his mother, who is knitting by the window, is going to the Lighthouse tomorrow, thus realising his profoundest dream. He shall go if it's fine, Mrs. Ramsay says. But it won't be fine, Mr. Ramsay declares. The day draws to a close, a day like many other days, made up of nothing; the children play, Lily Briscoe paints, Carmichael dozes and dreams, Tansley argues with his master Mr. Ramsay, Mrs. Ramsay knits and James cuts out his catalogue. The dinner gong summons them all to table to enjoy *boeuf en daube;* the children go to bed, the young people go off to the beach, Mr. and Mrs. Ramsay read. It will rain tomorrow. The evening is as empty and yet as full—and almost as long—as Clarissa Dalloway's day. Whereas the latter took its rhythm from the hours struck by Big Ben, here only the changing light in the garden marks the flow of time, and the unchanging noise of the waves holds the evening motionless. The characters, though their physical closeness creates a multiplicity of contacts, meanwhile withdraw each into his haunted solitude.

Then everybody comes indoors, the lights go out; and that night, that few hours' withdrawal, blends with the darkness and withdrawal of ten years' absence that flow over the empty house in twenty-five pages in which marriages, births and deaths are inscribed in parentheses. This is the second part which, after the personal reign of Duration, asserts the impersonal triumph of Time.

And as morning dawns after these two nights merged into one, corresponding to the evening that had flowed into them, James starts off for the Lighthouse with his sister Cam and his father, while Lily Briscoe sets up her easel where it must have stood ten years ago and

---

[34] Cf. AWD p. 104 (103), Feb. 12, 1927: ". . . I have to read *To the Lighthouse* tomorrow and Monday, straight through in print . . . ," and March 21, p. 106 (105): "Dear me, how lovely some parts of the *Lighthouse* are!" She compares her impressions on May 1st, p. 106 (105): ". . . I was disappointed when I read it through the first time. Later I liked it."

[35] Cf. AWD p. 104 (103): "Roger [Fry] it is clear did not like 'Time Passes.' "

[36] Cf. AWD pp. 106–7 (105): "I write however in the shadow of the damp cloud of *The Times Lit. Sup.* review. . . ."

[37] Cf. AWD, May 11 and May 16, 1927, p. 107 (106).

completes her painting, realising her vision at the same moment as James realises his dream. In the intensity of this second moment, Duration has revived and triumphed over Time, triumphed even over death since Mrs. Ramsay—who has died, in parentheses, under the reign of Time—haunts these pages with a presence that echoes the material permanence of the lighthouse.

When describing the birth and growth of this novel[38] I pointed out those features in its conception which seemed to relate it to Mrs. Dalloway. Even from the résumé given above, it is patent that this relationship has altered between the initial project and the final achievement. That Mrs. Ramsay has usurped the place originally assigned to her husband is a point to which I shall return. What interests us here is rather the way in which the central character dominates the book. Behind the account of Mrs. Ramsay's day we find no analysis of her feelings, no generalized interpretation of her attitudes; she is not the centre toward which all elements converge, as was the case with Mrs. Dalloway, in order to define her and strengthen her autonomous personality in face of the conflicts that divide her and the contradictory impressions that she arouses around her. On the contrary, by a kind of centrifugal process, Mrs. Ramsay radiates through the book, impregnating all the other characters.[39] And it is the relations that emanate from her personality, rather than the personality that emanates from these relations, that becomes the focus of interest in the book. This is an essential alteration of the initial project: in fact, Virginia Woolf has chosen the "wider slower book," thus escaping from the ghost of Mrs. Dalloway and from the danger of repetition.[40] By this choice she has committed herself to the path that she envisaged at the same time, the attempt "to split up emotions more completely." [41] Freed from the requirements of cohesion involved in the working out of a single character, she finds herself closer to the "purely psychological" conception of D. H. Lawrence.[42] The newness of this material, and the subtlety and rich-

---

[38] Cf. *supra*, p. 249.

[39] Cf. Lodwick Hartley, "Of Time and Mrs Woolf," *Sewanee Review*, XLVII, 1939, p. 235: "Change of tack. Instead of showing how many lives influence one character, it deals with the influence of one character on several lives."

[40] Cf. *supra*, p. 250.

[41] Cf. AWD p. 81 (80).

[42] Cf. D. H. Lawrence, Letter to Edward Garnett, June 5, 1914. Quoted by A. Huxley in *Stories, Essays and Poems*, Dent, London 1938, pp. 342: ". . . You must not look in my novel for the old stable *ego* of the character. There is another *ego*, according to whose action the individual is unrecognisable, and passes through, as it were, allotropic states which it needs a deeper sense than any we've been used to exercise, to discover are states of the same single radically unchanged element (Like as diamond and coal are the same pure single element of carbon)."

ness in it, have saved it from the other danger she apprehended: the
flatness of *Night and Day*.[43]

On the other hand the obsession with solitude, originally associated
with death, as in *Mrs Dalloway*,[44] loses its tragic character. Mr.
Ramsay's "We perished, each alone" retains under its declamatory
exaggeration a grievous truth and the pain of defeat. But although the
words become symbols, as the author is at pains to point out[45]—perhaps unnecessarily—they do not efface the memory of a different,
triumphant solitude, that of Mrs. Ramsay, the solitude and silence
into which the human being withdraws in order to become "a wedge-
shaped core of darkness," piercing to the heart of things in peace and
eternity.[46] This meditation of Mrs. Ramsay's, when she is alone for a
moment, the only time in the whole evening, seems to be the happiest
peak to which Virginia Woolf's thought ever attained. It corresponds
on the plane of sensibility and life to Lily Briscoe's vision,[47] which
completes it on the plane of rational and aesthetic thought. This
enables one to say that *To the Lighthouse,* deriving from *Mrs. Dalloway,* not only continues it but replies to the questions it asked.
Septimus died in solitude, and one guessed that Clarissa's sense of
communion might be a victory over that solitude and that death—
but one could only guess it. Clarissa answered the riddle that she
asked by her mere presence, which was unexplained except by the
words "she was." Mrs. Ramsay is the explicit expression of such a
presence. And at the same time the survival of that presence beyond
death, the dramatic character of which is relegated to the domain of
literature that obtrudes in Mr. Ramsay's declamations, abolishes
solitude and brings about the communion that Clarissa had only
suggested. Without denying those two ineluctable truths, solitude
and death, *To the Lighthouse* makes of them the two fundamental
experiences through which the human being, aspiring towards a single
truth, a single light, reaches these and fulfils himself.

This progress from one book to the next is the result neither of
literary artifice nor of abstract speculation. We have seen that Virginia
Woolf had really begun her novel in January 1926,[48] and it is on

[43] Cf. *supra*, p. 250, note 249.

[44] Cf. *supra*, p. 248.

[45] Cf. To the L pp. 227–8 (219): ". . . like everything else this strange morning the
words became symbols, wrote themselves all over the grey-green walls."

[46] Cf. To the L ch. I, section II, pp. 99–104 (95–100), particularly p. 99 (95): "To
be silent; to be alone. All the being and the doing, expansive, glittering, vocal,
evaporated; and one shrunk, with a sense of solemnity, to being oneself, a wedge-
shaped core of darkness, something invisible to others."

[47] Cf. To the L pp. 244–5 (235–6), 249 (240), 278–9 (269–70), 296–7 (288), 309–10
(299–300).

[48] Cf. *supra*, p. 251.

February 27th of that year that she writes in her diary the important
analysis of her "moments of vision." [49] The essential thing that lies
behind the appearances and the superficial individualities of Lily
Briscoe and Mrs. Ramsay is derived not from Julia Stephen or the
painter Vanessa,[50] but from Virginia Woolf herself. Does this mean
that this "elegiac" book[51] which inevitably drew its substance from
memories—even at the risk of becoming "sentimental"—slips into
that "self-centred dream" to which, at this period, the author was
accused of succumbing? [52] The boundary between one's present self
and one's past is so imprecise that they inevitably merge into one
another. Moreover, these two complementary realities are not mu-
tually exclusive; the first envelops and conceals the second. Virginia
Woolf had to pass through the present moment in order to recover
time past, without betraying either aspect of reality in her painting
of it. Her sister's opinion is reliable evidence:

> Nessa enthusiastic—a sublime, almost upsetting spectacle. She says it
> is an amazing portrait of mother; a supreme portrait painter; has lived
> in it; found the rising of the dead almost painful.[53]

Thus, in addition to whatever else it has become, the novel actually
is that evocation of the past that it sought to be. The close involvement of the author's whole being with that past is further confirmed
by the liberating function ascribed by Virginia Woolf to her book,
when on the ninety-sixth anniversary of her father's birth she writes:

> I used to think of him and mother daily: but writing the *Lighthouse*
> laid them in my mind.[54]

The Ambroses,[55] the Hilberrys,[56] Mrs. Dalloway were too sketchy,
too much mingled with foreign elements to free her from the burden
of all that she inherited from father and mother; only the completion
of their portraits could exhaust both the feeling that clung to them
and the literary temptation that gave a parasitical life to their memories.

It remains to be asked why the respective positions of Mr. and
Mrs. Ramsay have been inverted. *A Writer's Diary* says nothing about

---

[40] Cf. *supra*, ch. III, pp. 111–12.
[50] Leonard Woolf has suggested that the analysis of the painter's processes in Lily
Briscoe is based on Vanessa Stephen, who married Clive Bell.
[51] Cf. *supra*, p. 249.
[52] Cf. *supra*, ch. III, p. 65, and AWD pp. 120–1 (118–9).
[53] AWD p. 107 (106).
[54] Cf. *supra*, ch. III, p. 62, and AWD p. 138 (135).
[55] In *The Voyage Out.*
[56] In *Night and Day.*

this alteration, which seems significant enough to justify some comment, even if the reasons adduced remain mere hypotheses.

Mr. Ramsay, it must be admitted, is not a sympathetic character; his originality, his anxiety and loneliness, his need for admiration and sympathy do not suffice to redeem his intransigent positivism, his selfishness and brusquerie. No doubt it is of the unflattering side of her portrait that Virginia Woolf is thinking when she writes: "People will say I am irreverent. . . ." [57] The picture of Leslie Stephen in her *Times* article of 1932[58] is certainly recognizable as Mr. Ramsay, but in a gentler and more lovable form. If we compare these two portraits with the one that emerges from Annan's book[59] we realize that both are true. Their difference is that which separates an intimate relationship from a more impersonal acquaintance. Mr. Ramsay is the father figure which had to be exorcised; it was his despotism in all its forms, over mind and heart, that had to be overthrown. And no doubt the domination he exercised over his entourage gave rise to the initial idea that he should dominate the book. But the element of antagonism between the author and her protagonist eclipsed their affinities, and would have condemned the book to a certain externality, acceptable perhaps for the short, swift book originally planned, but incompatible with the longer, slower book eventually chosen.

Of Virginia Woolf's relations with her mother we know little. Yet from the violence of the shock which the 13-year-old girl felt at her loss[60] we may conclude that between mother and daughter there were certain deep affinities which became fixed and idealized at the same time through this premature death. *To the Lighthouse,* being an elegy, could only have as its central figure a being wholly and unreservedly loved. Moreover, if Leslie Stephen could represent that rational quest of truth and that feeling of solitude which the author sought to express, only Julia Stephen could represent that unfailing intuition, that sensibility, that gift of sympathy which, for Virginia Woolf, are the supreme human qualities, those which give a person that intensely radiant power that illuminates our darkness like a lighthouse beam. Finally, in this novel which is above all an analysis of the relations that connect and mingle human beings beneath the words and gestures whose value as communication is so inadequate, a

---

[57] AWD p. 106 (105).

[58] "Leslie Stephen," published in *The Captain's Death Bed*, pp. 67–71 (69–75).

[59] Noel Annan, *Leslie Stephen*, Macgibbon & Kee, London, 1951, and Harvard University Press, 1952.

[60] It was following the death of her mother that V. W. had her first nervous breakdown and tried to commit suicide. Cf. Rantavaara, *V. W. and Bloomsbury*, 1953. p. 106.

medium was needed who could scarcely be imagined save as a woman endowed with "some secret sense, fine as air." [61] No doubt Virginia Woolf would be the first to protest against the artificial element in the traditional opposition between men's and women's natures. Yet she usually respects their broad lines, and in *To the Lighthouse* she stresses the opposition and exploits it.[62] And one can even see in this exploitation a certain bias which reflects tendencies that were strongly marked in her: on the one hand, her feminism, in the broad sense of the word, which might be defined as a defiant belief in woman's superiority in the quest for truth and the almost occult knowledge of life: on the other hand, a kind of nostalgic yearning for a relation between women, opposed to love between man and woman. I have tried to define, with all the prudence necessitated by the lack of precise documents, Virginia Woolf's conception of love[63]; Ruth Gruber[64] has pointed out the interest she showed in Lesbianism, as witness the relations between Sally Seton and Clarissa Dalloway, Elizabeth and Miss Kilman, and the ambiguity of Orlando. While writing *Mrs. Dalloway,* she drops a hint in her diary:

> Yesterday I had tea in Mary's room and saw the red lighted tugs go past and heard the swish of the river Mary: in black with lotus leaves round her neck. If one could be friendly with women, what a pleasure —the relationship so secret and private compared with relations with men. Why not write about it? Truthfully? [65]

Without seeking to extract from this passage more than it contains, one cannot help being aware of the emotional burden it betrays and the uneasiness that emanates from it. No doubt it is merely something instantaneous, as fleeting as Sally's kiss on Clarissa's lips or Lily Briscoe's impulse of affection for Mrs. Ramsay. No doubt, these lines only express aspiration and longing, but at the same time they admit concealment and tabu. In the summer of 1926, when *To the Lighthouse* was nearing completion, Virginia Woolf saw a great deal of Victoria Sackville-West,[66] as she did again the following summer, when the idea of *Orlando* occurred to her.[67] In January 1927 she went

[61] To the L p. 303 (294).
[62] Cf. Mary Electa Kelsey, "V. W. and the She-condition," *Sewanee Review*, Oct.-Dec. 1931, esp. pp. 433 and 442.
[63] Cf. *supra*, ch. III, pp. 66–70.
[64] Ruth Gruber, *V. W. A Study* (Kölner Anglist Arbeiten XXIV, Leipzig, Tauchnitz, 1935, p. 100). Quoted by Rantavaara, p. 148.
[65] AWD pp. 68–9 (67).
[66] Cf. AWD p. 99 (97) (quoted *supra*, p. 251, note 256).
[67] Cf. AWD pp. 110 (108), 113–14 (112).

to Knole.[68] And it was in September 1928, after the publication of *Orlando,* that the two friends went to France together, by themselves.[69] The biographical enigma posed by these facts, these allusions, these literary transpositions can only be answered—apart from the *Orlando* frolic which has already been referred to[70]—by Mrs. Ramsay's reflection: "Love had a thousand shapes." [71] And this assertion, while it answers our enquiry, however inadequately, also replies to the doubt that flashed through Rachel twenty years earlier, when she thought about her feeling for Helen Ambrose, about Richard Dalloway's kiss, or about any other man she might meet later on: ". . . she could not possibly want only one human being." [72] *Orlando* and *The Waves,* later, assert the same conviction, which moreover is complementary to those intermittences of the heart to which Virginia Woolf's psychology allotted so important a place.

The analysis of the married relation which Blackstone, for instance, tends to consider the chief focus of interest in *To the Lighthouse,*[73] is in fact only one particular case of the instability and complexity of our feelings. The paragraph in her Diary on "The married relation," [74] written in the summer of 1926, suggests that by then, after fourteen years of marriage, Virginia Woolf had decided to take her bearings. However, if certain elements of personal experience have unquestionably been transposed into the novel, this has a significance that goes far beyond what it can tell us about the Ramsays or the Rayleys, and it is at least as plausible to take the Diary paragraph as a hybrid comment, scribbled in the margin of the book and of life, rather than as the sign of a dominant preoccupation underlying the book.

Since I propose to study the problem of Time[75] and the question of structure[76] elsewhere, I shall merely allude to the importance of these two points, which I have tried to bring out in my summary of *To the Lighthouse.* I shall only mention that the change of tone, of style, of movement in the second part caused the author some anxi-

[68] Cf. AWD p. 103 (102), Jan. 23, 1927.

[69] Cf. V. Sackville-West in *Horizon,* May 1941, Vol. III, no. 17, pp. 318–24, and AWD p. 133 (131): "I went to Burgundy with Vita . . . on 26th September when I went to France."

[70] Cf. *supra,* ch. III, p. 79.

[71] To the L, p. 295 (280). The phrase occurs in Lily Briscoe's interior monologue and is both personal and reminiscent of Mrs Ramsay's words; it echoes Mrs Ramsay's thought, p. 162 (157) ". . . one of those unclassified affections of which there are so many."

[72] Cf. VO p. 370 (302).

[73] Cf. Bernard Blackstone, *V. W.* pp. 100 and 113.

[74] Cf. *supra,* ch. III, p. 70.

[75] Cf. *infra,* ch. VI, section 3.

[76] Cf. *infra,* ch. VI, section 5.

ety.[77] Perhaps Roger Fry's disapproval[78] was partly responsible; unless it was her awareness of the audacity represented by this technical process and the inevitable hostility it would arouse among critics and readers. It is not surprising to find Arnold Bennett condemning this second part.[79] There is no doubt that the virtuosity of these pages emphasizes their strangeness. Yet they are neither irrelevant ornament nor a purely technical device. Their aim is precisely to set in the very centre of the book, in a significant fashion, the essential, ambiguous protagonist: Time-Duration. Whereas under the aspect of Duration it plays its role in the two other sections, discreetly merged into the consciousness of the *dramatis personae,* in this second part, under the aspect of Time, it achieves its inhuman task as cosmic agent.

No doubt Virginia Woolf implicitly admits a heterogeneity, the dangers of which she did not minimize: "The lyric portions of *To the Lighthouse* are collected in the 10-year lapse and don't interfere with the text so much as usual." But declaring in the next sentence that the book fetched its circle pretty completely this time,[80] she asserts thereby that its heterogeneity, far from interrupting the line of the work, is an integral part of it. Without contesting that the dual nature of the tone is evidence of a duality in the author's personality, what has been called (by R. Las Vergnas) her androgynousness, I should like to suggest that *To the Lighthouse,* by its structure, its movement, as also by its essential subject, attempts to resolve that duality, and that *The Waves* only develops and carries to the limits of their potential the resources of style and composition which are exploited here.[81]

Such as it is, retaining enough traditional elements and characters and a semblance of a plot to satisfy the common reader, yet brimming with inward life and with a lyricism which give it a density characteristic of Virginia Woolf, *To the Lighthouse,* by the synthesis which it achieves and the balance it maintains between contradictory tendencies, won the favour of the reading public[82] and at the same time, if it did not gain unanimous approval from the critics, was at

[77] Cf. AWD p. 107 (105): "I am anxious about 'Time Passes.' "

[78] Cf. AWD p. 104 (103): "Roger it is clear did not like 'Time Passes.' "

[79] Cf. A. Bennett in *The Evening Standard,* June 23, 1927. ". . . The middle part does not succeed. It is a short cut, but a short cut that does not get you anywhere. . . . I doubt the very difficult business of conveying the idea of the passage of a very considerable amount of time can be completed by means of a device . . . (it) has to be conveyed gradually without any direct insistence—in the manner of life itself."

[80] AWD p. 100 (98).

[81] Cf. *infra,* ch. V, pp. 282–302.

[82] In 1951, 11 editions of To the L as against 7 of Mrs D and JR and 6 of VO, N & D and The W.

least granted indulgence by some who unhesitatingly condemn her other novels.[83]

[83] Cf. Conrad Aiken, "The Novel as a Work of Art," *Dial*, July 1927; Orlo Williams, *"To the Lighthouse," The Monthly Criterion*, July 1927, vol. VI, 1, p. 28; D. M. Hoare, *Some Studies in the Modern Novel*, 1933, p. 61; Robert Peel, "Virginia Woolf," *The Criterion*, Oct. 1933, vol. XIII, 50, p. 91; Martin Turnell, "Virginia Woolf," *Horizon*, VI, July 1942, pp. 53–4. Among critics generally favourable to V. W., E. M. Forster (*Virginia Woolf*, The Rede Lecture, Cambridge Univ. Press, 1941, p. 14), David Daiches (*Virginia Woolf*, New Directions, 1942, pp. 95–6; Nicholson & Watson, London, p. 92) and I. Rantavaara (*Virginia Woolf and Bloomsbury*, Helsinki, 1953, p. 116) assert their preference for *To the Lighthouse*.

PART TWO

View Points

Arnold Kettle: Mr. Bennett and Mrs. Woolf

In what sense may life be said, in *To the Lighthouse,* not to escape? In the sense, perhaps, that there is nothing secondhand about this novel, that the convention in which it is written permits Virginia Woolf to convey with extraordinary precision a certain intimate quality of felt life. The dinner scene which is at the centre of the novel is a piece of writing worth comparing with, say, Galsworthy's description of dinner at Swithin Forsyte's in the early part of *The Man of Property.* Galsworthy's dinner is well described; we get a sense of what kind of room Swithin's dining-room is, of what each of the characters sitting round the table is like, of the social interplay going on throughout the meal and the quality of the saddle of mutton. But the effect is, compared with Virginia Woolf's, a surface effect. We are not made aware of the moment-by-moment texture of feeling, the intricate pattern of reaction, the wispish, wayward flitting of consciousness, the queer changes in tempo of the responses, the *taste* of the food, the sudden violent swoops of emotion and the strange, enhanced significance of outside, inanimate, casual things, a shadow on the table, the pattern of the cloth.

In the description (if it is not too intractable a word) of the dinner in *To the Lighthouse* a dimension is introduced which in Galsworthy's writing is altogether absent. And that dimension—let us call it the impression of the momentary texture of experience—has the effect which Virginia Woolf was seeking when she used the words "luminous halo" to describe life. There is a luminous quality in the general effect of *To the Lighthouse* which is what gives the novel its particular value. These people may not be very interesting, neither their activities nor their mental pre-occupations may concern us very much when we abstract and think about them; but they are alive. They breathe the air, they catch the fragrance of the flowers or the tang of the sea, they eat real food, they *know* one another. Whatever they are they are not cardboard figures or puppets or caricatures (we have come to the furthest point from the comedy of humours); and

"Mr. Bennett and Mrs. Woolf." From An Introduction to the English Novel *by Arnold Kettle (London: Hutchinson Publishing Group, 1961), Vol. II, Part III, 103–5. Copyright 1953 by Arnold Kettle. Reprinted by permission of the publisher.*

because they are in this physical—one might almost say primitive—
sense alive they have a kind of resilience which is rare in literature.
Robert Liddell has said well: "The truth is perhaps this: while we
know the characters of Miss Austen as we know our friends (if we are
abnormally observant), we know Mrs. Woolf's character as we know
ourselves." This is a reference of course to the quality and not the
quantity of knowledge involved. The effect of *To the Lighthouse* is
the absolute antithesis of flatness.

And yet . . . ? Having said this, having relished what is in this
novel unique and exquisite, have we not missed out what is most
important of all? Is it right to resist the temptation, after one has
finished *To the Lighthouse* and remained for a while sensitive to its
spell, to slam it with as vulgar a gesture as one can muster and permit
to fall the brutal words: "So what?"

The trouble with *To the Lighthouse,* it seems to me, is the quite
simple and quite fundamental trouble that it is, when all is said, not
about anything very interesting or important. That, of course, is
putting it too simply and leaving oneself wide open to some obvious
rejoinders. In one sense all life is, from the writer's point of view,
equally important and when a novelist achieves an effect of expression
which we feel to be "good" that is that. The effect of *To the Lighthouse* is something new in literature (and we cannot say that of the
novels of Bennett or Galsworthy); in the moments of enjoyment of
the book we experience something we have not experienced before
and our sensibility is, by that experience, refined. In this sense Virginia Woolf may justly be regarded as a finer, more truly artistic writer
than any of the Edwardian novelists we have discussed. But that is
not the only thing to be said.

D. S. Savage, in an essay on Virginia Woolf, has written:

> The distinguishing feature of Virginia Woolf's apprehension of life
> lies . . . in its passivity; and furthermore, she subscribed unwittingly
> . . . to a view of life which placed a primary emphasis upon the object.
> One recalls the passive function ascribed to the mind ("The mind re-
> ceives a myriad impressions") and the atomistic conception of experience
> ("From all sides they come, an incessant *shower of atoms*") revealed in the
> essay "Modern Fiction". . . . Virginia Woolf's search for "significance"
> on the primitive level of primary sensational perceptions . . . was chi-
> merical from the beginning. And, indeed it is a typical feature of the
> characters of her novels to be altogether lacking in the capacity for dis-
> criminating within experience. They are passively caught up in the
> streams of events, of "Life," of their own random perceptions.

I think Mr. Savage underrates Virginia Woolf's powers but he seems
to me to make here an essential point. Upon what is this subtle apparatus of sensibility after all exercised? Upon what vision of the

world, what scale of human values, is it based? What is lacking in
To the Lighthouse is a basic conflict, a framework of human effort.
What does Lily Briscoe's vision really amount to? In what sense is
the episode in the boat between James and Mr. Ramsay really a
culmination of their earlier relationship?

Lodwick Hartley: Of Time and Mrs. Woolf

Mrs. Woolf's art is a pure art that has been attained through a
somewhat dogged rigidity of purpose. She has rejected the sentimentality and the moralizing of the Victorians, as well as the social
propagandizing of her contemporaries. "I believe that all novels . . .
deal with character," she wrote in "Mr. Bennett and Mrs. Brown,"
one of her finest critical essays, "and that it is to express character—
not to preach doctrines, sing songs, or celebrate the glories of the
British Empire, that the form of the novel . . . has been evolved."
Emphasis on characterization has, of course, always been the basis of
realistic fiction; but Mrs. Woolf goes beyond the traditional emphasis.
Her characters are rarely objective in the sense of the psychological
case-history or the painted canvas. Her theory of characterization—
subtle, fresh, and poetic though it assuredly is—prescribes very definite
bounds, in spite of its seeming limitlessness. Bernard speaks for Mrs.
Woolf in the epilogue to *The Waves:* "I am not one person; I am
many people; I do not know who I am—Jimmy, Susan, Neville,
Rhoda, or Louis: or how to distinguish my life from theirs." Therefore, in *The Waves,* we are to assume, it is in the merging of the six
characters, not in the individual figures that one finds the pattern of
life itself, the Everyman. The same idea may be used as the defense
of the general tendency of Mrs. Woolf's characters to merge into the
pattern of life in which we find them. The idea is so striking that it
is likely to make a rapid conquest of one's credence. But away from
Mrs. Woolf's spell one may find cause to wonder whether this annihilation of the microcosm, this achievement of Nirvana, is not both
specious and precious. Admitting that it does throw light on a phase
of human experience, one will probably find that as a device of
characterization it has its disadvantages. Mrs. Woolf's characters, for
all their charm, have a way of staying on the surface of one's consciousness; they never eat their way into the very fiber of one's being as
great literary characters have a way of doing. Jacob, Mrs. Dalloway,
Mrs. Ramsay, and Eleanor Pargiter are not made of quite the same

"*Of Time and Mrs. Woolf*" by Lodwick Hartley. From Sewanee **Review** *47*
(*1939*): 237-39. *Reprinted by permission of The University of the South.*

stuff that went into Stephen Dedalus, Isabel Archer, Mrs. Morel, Mrs. Forrester, and Eugene Gant.

The central philosophical problem of Mrs. Woolf's characters is the search for the meaning of life. "What is the meaning of life?" asks Lily Briscoe in *To the Lighthouse*. "Where am I going?" echoes Eleanor Pargiter in *The Years*. Indeed, the problem is important enough, but Mrs. Woolf makes no attempt to answer with any degree of assurance. "Perhaps the great revelation never did come," she wrote in *To the Lighthouse*. "Instead there were little daily miracles, illuminations, matches struck unexpectedly in the dark; here was one. This, that and the other; herself and Charles Tansley and the breaking wave; Mrs. Ramsay bringing them together; Mrs. Ramsay saying, 'Life stand still here'; Mrs. Ramsay making of the moment something permanent—this was of the nature of a revelation." The only stability, Mrs. Woolf leads us to believe, is the continuity of life. This, obviously, is only another way of saying that only change is changeless. Shorn of the rich imagery and faultless style with which she skillfully dresses it, Mrs. Woolf's philosophy seems to run in this manner: Where are we going? We don't know; but we are *going,* and that is something. Admittedly, I am handling Mrs. Woolf a little roughly here, but I am merely trying to discover whether her thinking represents patisserie or meat, whether it should not better be served as a delicacy for the tea table than as the entrée for the evening meal.

But perhaps it is the part of Philistinism to blame Mrs. Woolf because she presents no challenging philosophy and to point out that, stripped of their subtlety of presentation, her conclusions are commonplace. Perhaps we have no right to demand of the artist affirmation or negation. It would be too bad to clutter up literature with Leith Walks and Everlasting Yeas. It may require no more real mental effort to arrive at a fatalism like Hardy's than it does to admit that life is an enigma. But in the novel, it seems to me, the conclusions themselves are not the thing. What really matters is the vitality that the work of art gets through the struggle of the author or of the characters toward a conclusion of some sort. The element of struggle is not entirely absent from Mrs. Woolf's novels, but it is made subliminal. Presented through overtones, implications, and suggestions, it is hardly central enough to give a vitality of its own.

F. R. Leavis: After To the Lighthouse

Mrs. Woolf's best novel, it is pretty generally agreed, is To the Lighthouse; to me, as to others, it is the only good one—the only one in which her talent fulfils itself in a satisfactory achievement. The substance of this novel was provided directly by life—in a more vulgar sense of the word than that given it above: we know enough about Leslie Stephen, the novelist's father, and his family to know that there is a large measure of direct transcription. We can see a clear relation between this fact and the unique success of To the Lighthouse among her novels. Mrs. Woolf's decision to have "no plot, no comedy, no tragedy, no love-interest or catastrophe in the accepted style" was perhaps to this extent justified, that she hadn't interests rich and active enough to justify what she was rejecting; but neither, we have to conclude, had she interests adequate to the problem of supplying substitutes. By way of eliminating any unduly pejorative suggestions of "accepted style" we may adduce the Conrad she admired—the great artist whose essential and successful concern was indisputably with that which Mr. Bennett, "with his magnificent apparatus for catching life," seemed to miss—"whether we call it life or spirit, truth or reality"; the contrast brings out how little of human experience—how little of life—comes within Mrs. Woolf's scope.

The envelope enclosing her dramatized sensibilities may be "semi-transparent"; but it seems to shut out all the ranges of experience accompanying those kinds of preoccupation, volitional and moral, with an external world which are not felt primarily as preoccupation with one's consciousness of it. The preoccupation with intimating "significance" in fine shades of consciousness, together with the unremitting play of visual imagery, the "beautiful" writing and the lack of moral interest and interest in action, give the effect of something closely akin to a sophisticated aestheticism. (There is also the Aesthetic brooding wistfulness about the passage of time.)

Weaknesses of this kind (for weaknesses they are, though triumphs may be won out of them) have, we know, their fostering conditions in the relation of the artist to modern society. A sensitive mind whose main interests are not endorsed by the predominant interests of the world it lives in, and whose talent and professional skill seem to have no real public importance, is naturally apt to cultivate (if

"After To the Lighthouse" by F. R. Leavis. From Scrutiny 10, no. 1 (June 1941): 297–98. Reprinted by permission of the publisher.

this is the right word) the "bubble of the private consciousness." Not that Mrs. Woolf hadn't her congenial and applauding social-cultural milieu. She belonged, of course, to the original Bloomsbury, the Bloomsbury of Clive Bell's *Civilisation* and Lytton Strachey's wit (some of her essays are in his cheapest manner, and one can seldom feel quite safe from the communal note). A milieu that so often reminds us of its potency in the work of as distinguished a writer as E. M. Forster must be held accountable for a great deal in the development—or failure to develop—of Virginia Woolf. The general nature of its operation may be seen in the Preface and text of *Orlando*, the work that followed *To the Lighthouse*, and after which the discouraging signs multiplied steadily to the end.

Elizabeth Drew: To the Lighthouse

To the Lighthouse was published in 1927, the fifth of Virginia Woolf's eight novels, and is generally considered the finest; the one in which she brought her method to its delicate perfection. It is indeed a wonderful piece of workmanship. Her foundation of ideas is "clamped together" in the symbolic structure she chose to suggest it. At the same time the "feathery, evanescent" nature of consciousness— the permeation of the present by the past, the outer by the inner, the currents uniting personalities and dividing them, the moments when things come together and fall apart, the intermingling of the emotions and the senses, all the mazy motions of reverie—all this is vividly revealed. Her characters all come to life, as we see into their own minds and into their images in the minds of others. We constantly recognize the truth of her psychological insights. Her mastery of her medium and her riches of concrete metaphorical suggestion are everywhere. Unquestionably she was a "professional," evolving a new form of fiction and creating a masterpiece in it.

Any criticism must center on how much of "felt life" this form of fiction is capable of holding. "I want to put practically everything in . . . but made transparent." What does Virginia Woolf *not* put in? In one of her reveries Mrs. Ramsay meditates on some of the terrible aspects of life:

> There is no reason, order, justice: but suffering, death, the poor. There was no treachery too base for the world to commit; she knew that. No happiness lasted; she knew that.

"To the Lighthouse." *From* The Novel: A Modern Guide to Fifteen English Masterpieces *by Elizabeth Drew. (New York: Dell Publishing Co., Inc., 1963), pp. 278–89. Reprinted by permission of the publisher.*

None of these things enters the book; but then Jane Austen also excluded all powerful emotion. Virginia Woolf provides no comprehensive social structure to acquiesce in or rebel from; but Emily Brontë excluded that too. No, the one thing we really miss is the lack of any progressive action involving moral and emotional choices and decisions; any pattern of relationships being shaped and directed by such action. In all the other books we have discussed, we watch the characters *making* their lives; in *To the Lighthouse* we see very clearly what they *have made* of them, but they are forced to remain static; it is all expansion without progression.

This, however, is how Virginia Woolf sees life. James, in the boat going to the Lighthouse, "began to search among the infinite series of impressions which time had laid down, leaf upon leaf, fold upon fold, softly, incessantly upon his brain." To Virginia Woolf it is this ceaseless fall of the atoms upon the consciousness that creates human identity. In the book we live among these myriad impressions, from the past and in the immediate present, which have patterned personality and from which the texture of experience is woven. Our insights are sharpened, our senses delighted. The moral values are there too; we look through the transparent "luminous halo" and know in a general way what Virginia Woolf sees as the springs of human good and human evil. We believe in the moments of heightened consciousness which seem to transcend time, and accept, again in a general way, the analogy with the "wholeness, harmony and radiance" of a work of art. But what we are shown lacks substance and particularity. We miss the conflict of wills and the dynamic movement which the method forbids; reactions can never be as powerful as actions, or impressions as events. In *The Portrait of a Lady* or *A Portrait of the Artist* we live a great deal in the inner world of consciousness, and important themes are embodied in recurrent imagery and symbolic structure. But these are reinforced by an interplay of action creating character, and character originating action, and are carried forward with seeming inevitability toward a resolution. The pure "stream of consciousness" method excludes this, and that is probably why it has not survived. It founders on that bedrock necessity which E. M. Forster laments though accepts: "The novel must tell a story."

José Ortega y Gasset: Imaginary Psychology

The material of the novel, we were saying, is, above all, imaginary psychology. It is not easy to explain in a few words what this means. The current belief is that psychological phenomena, like the phenomena of experimental physics, obey factual laws. If this is so, all the novelist can do is to observe and to copy the real processes in existing souls. But he cannot invent psychological processes and construct souls as the mathematician constructs geometrical figures. Yet the enjoyment of novels presupposes exactly this.

When a novelist expounds a psychological process he does not expect us to accept it as something that has actually happened—who would guarantee its reality?—but he trusts that it possesses an inner evidence, an evidence akin to that which makes mathematics possible. And let it not be said that the psychological development he describes seems convincing when it coincides with cases we have witnessed in life. An awkward thing it would be if the novelist had to rely on the chance experiences of this or that reader of his. Rather we recall that one of the peculiar attractions Dostoevski's work used to hold for us lay in the unfamiliar behavior of his personages. Small chance there is indeed that a reader in Sevilla should ever in his life have met people as chaotic and turbulent as the Karamasoffs. And yet, dull though he may be, the psychic mechanism of those souls seems to him as cogent and evident as the steps of a mathematical proof which uses dimensions never seen by human eyes.

There exists in psychology, just as in mathematics, an evidence a priori. Because of this in either field imaginary construction is possible. Where only facts are subject to laws but no laws obtain that regulate the imagination it is impossible to construct. Any attempt to do so can be no more than an arbitrary caprice.

Because this is not recognized the psychology in a novel is taken to be identical with that of real life, and it is assumed that the author can do nothing but copy reality. So coarse a reasoning lies at the bottom of what is currently called "realism." I cannot now discuss this involved term which I have been careful always to use in quotation marks to render it suspect. Its incongruity will clearly transpire when

———————
"Imaginary Psychology." From The Dehumanization of Art and Other Essays on Art, Culture, and Literature *by José Ortega y Gasset (Princeton, N.J.: Princeton University [Princeton Paperback], 1968), pp. 93–95. Copyright © 1968, revised edition, by Princeton University Press. Reprinted by permission of the publisher.*

we observe that it does not even apply to the very works from which it allegedly derives. The personages of those works are almost all of them so different from those we meet in our own environment that, even supposing they were copied from existing persons, we should not recognize them as such. People in a novel need not be like real ones, it is enough that they are possible. And this psychology of possible human minds, which I have called imaginary psychology, is the only one that matters to the novel. That a novel may, apart from this, be concerned with giving a psychological interpretation of actual social types and environments can provide an additional piquancy, but it is not essential. (One of the points I am leaving untouched is that the novel lends itself more easily than any other literary form to absorbing elements alien to art. *Within* the novel almost anything fits: science, religion, sociology, aesthetic criticism—if only it is ultimately derealized and confined within the inner world of the novel; i.e., if it remains without actual and effective validity. In other words, a novel can contain as much sociology as it desires, but the novel itself cannot be sociological. The dose of alien elements a book can bear, lastly, depends on the author's capability of dissolving them in the atmosphere of the novel as such. But this subject obviously belongs to casuistry, and I drop it terrified.)

This possibility of constructing human souls is perhaps the major asset of future novels. Everything points in this direction. The interest in the outer mechanism of the plot is today reduced to a minimum. All the better: the novel must now revolve about the superior interest emanating from the inner mechanism of the personages. Not in the invention of plots but in the invention of interesting characters lies the best hope of the novel.

Herman Melville: Quite an Original

"QUITE AN ORIGINAL:" A phrase, we fancy, rather oftener used by the young, or the unlearned, or the untraveled, than by the old, or the well-read, or the man who has made the grand tour. Certainly, the sense of originality exists at its highest in an infant, and probably at its lowest in him who has completed the circle of the sciences.

As for original characters in fiction, a grateful reader will, on meeting with one, keep the anniversary of that day. True, we sometimes hear of an author who, at one creation, produces some two or three

---

"Quite an Original." From The Confidence-Man *by Herman Melville.*

score such characters; it may be possible. But they can hardly be original in the sense that Hamlet is, or Don Quixote, or Milton's Satan.
That is to say, they are not, in a thorough sense, original at all. They
are novel, or singular, or striking, or captivating, or all four at once.

More likely, they are what are called odd characters; but for that,
are no more original, than what is called an odd genius, in his way,
is. But, if original, whence came they? Or where did the novelist
pick them up?

Where does any novelist pick up any character? For the most part,
in town, to be sure. Every great town is a kind of man-show, where
the novelist goes for his stock, just as the agriculturist goes to the
cattle-show for his. But in the one fair, new species of quadrupeds are
hardly more rare, than in the other are new species of characters—that
is, original ones. Their rarity may still the more appear from this,
that, while characters, merely singular, imply but singular forms, so to
speak, original ones, truly so, imply original instincts.

In short, a due conception of what is to be held for this sort of
personage in fiction would make him almost as much of a prodigy
there, as in real history is a new law-giver, a revolutionizing philosopher, or the founder of a new religion.

In nearly all the original characters, loosely accounted such in works
of invention, there is discernible something prevailingly local, or of
the age; which circumstance, of itself, would seem to invalidate the
claim, judged by the principles here suggested.

Furthermore, if we consider, what is popularly held to entitle characters in fiction to being deemed original, is but something personal
—confined to itself. The character sheds not its characteristic on its
surroundings, whereas, the original character, essentially such, is like
a revolving Drummond light, raying away from itself all around it—
everything is lit by it, everything starts up to it (mark how it is with
Hamlet), so that, in certain minds, there follows upon the adequate
conception of such a character, an effect, in its way, akin to that
which in Genesis attends upon the beginning of things.

For much the same reason that there is but one planet to one orbit,
so can there be but one such original character to one work of invention. Two would conflict to chaos. In this view, to say that there are
more than one to a book, is good presumption there is none at all.
But for new, singular, striking, odd, eccentric, and all sorts of enter-
taining and instructive characters, a good fiction may be full of them.
To produce such characters, an author, beside other things, must
have seen much, and seen through much: to produce but one original
character, he must have had much luck.

There would seem but one point in common between this sort of phenomenon in fiction and all other sorts: it cannot be born in the author's imagination—it being as true in literature as in zoology, that all life is from the egg.

Josephine O'Brien Schaefer: To the Lighthouse: 1927

Why does Augustus Carmichael distrust Mrs. Ramsay? Why did Minta Doyle's mother say something that reminds Mrs. Ramsay of another woman's accusation that she was "robbing her of her daughter's affections"? Why does Paul Rayley feel, immediately after his engagement, that he "would go straight to Mrs. Ramsay, because he felt somehow that she was the person who had made him do it"? Cut off from the wider world of action available to men, Mrs. Ramsay finds no range for the exertion of her powers and inevitably employs them in personal domination. It is this aspect of her character that keeps Augustus Carmichael at a distance. His shrinking hurts her but, as she says to herself, "not cleanly, not rightly"; for it makes her feel that "all this desire of hers to give, to help, was vanity." His withdrawal makes her "aware of the pettiness of some part of her, and of human relations how flawed they are, how despicable, how self-seeking at their best." Lily Briscoe recognizes how Mrs. Ramsay's pity for men is related to her desire for a suitable arena for her own activities. Hearing Mrs. Ramsay speak to William Bankes, Lily wonders,

> Why does she pity him? For that was the impression she gave, when she told him that his letters were in the hall. Poor William Bankes she seemed to be saying, as if her own weariness had been partly pitying people, and the life in her, her resolve to live again, had been stirred by pity. And it was not true, Lily thought; it was one of those misjudgments of hers that seemed to be instinctive and to arise from some need of her own rather than of other people's.

Virginia Woolf sees possibilities for humor in Mrs. Ramsay's small world and limited view. She turns the matter into a physical disability; three times at least Mrs. Ramsay is described as shortsighted. She sees what is right in front of her: the man putting up billboards, her husband and children, the two figures immediately before her on a lawn.

"To the Lighthouse: *1927*." From The Three-Fold Nature of Reality in the Novels of Virginia Woolf *by Josephine O'Brien Schaefer (The Hague: Mouton & Company 1965), pp. 123–25. Copyright © 1965 by Josephine O'Brien Schaefer. Reprinted by permission of the author.*

Deftly the deficiency in sight and the practical exertion of will are
made correspondent:

> Ah, but was that not Lily Briscoe strolling along with William Bankes?
> She focussed her short-sighted eyes upon the backs of the retreating
> couple. Yes, indeed it was. Did that not mean that they would marry?
> Yes, it must! What an admirable idea! They must marry.

And yet it is this particular human being, Mrs. Ramsay, compact of
great strength and weakness, whose presence gives shape and coher-
ence to the famous dinner party; "And directly she went a sort of
disintegration set in. . . ." The candles, the fragrant and delicious
Boeuf en Daube, the family, the friends, combine to form a moment
in life which resembles in its beauty and completeness a work of art.
That dining room becomes a lighthouse as the group grows conscious
of being a party.

> Now all the candles were lit, and the faces on both sides of the table
> were brought nearer by the candle light, and composed, as they had not
> been in the twilight, into a party round a table, for the night was now
> shut off by panes of glass, which, far from giving any accurate view
> of the outside world, rippled it so strangely that here, inside the room,
> seemed to be order and dry land. There, outside, a reflection in which
> things wavered and vanished, waterily.

The real lighthouse of the novel, therefore, is the one which Mrs.
Ramsay carefully sets glowing and which illuminates a space of life
even after her death. This illumination becomes a triumph of the
human spirit as Virginia Woolf recounts the dead beginnings of this
memorable party. The mood of utter emptiness with which the meal
commences, Mrs. Ramsay's sense "of being past everything, through
everything, out of everything," is a mood very like Mrs. Dalloway's
when she reads the note from Richard upon her return home. By
means of formulas, of conventional chatter, Mrs. Ramsay sets about
lifting that gloom. As always Virginia Woolf shows what effort is
required to resist the attractions of oblivion and return to life. Even
Mrs. Ramsay, a guardian of life, finds it difficult to summon her
powers and take up the burden of living again. In her dead mood she
sees the joyous meal that may occur if she takes the immense trouble
to set about creating it. Virginia Woolf compares her to a sailor who
"not without weariness sees the wind fill his sail and yet hardly wants
to be off again and thinks how, had the ship sunk, he would have
whirled round and round and found rest on the floor of the sea."
She rouses herself and with much effort rekindles the lighthouse,
making it shine so brilliantly that ten years later Lily Briscoe, James
and Cam see by its light again.

John Hawley Roberts: Toward Virginia Woolf

After *Mrs. Dalloway* came *To the Lighthouse* (1927). Again the attempt is to capture "the spirit of life itself." But here, having already given us in *Mrs. Dalloway,* under the guise of various people, a cross-section of life's pattern, Mrs. Woolf narrows down her field to one all-important factor: the discovery of what it is that gives to the design its sense of reality. Having already denied that reality lies in external details, she now denounces another Edwardian principle—that concept of time by which an object is at one moment presumably the same as it is at another moment. This had already occupied her attention in *Mrs. Dalloway,* where the clock-time of one day yields to the power of memory, which can not only make the past as vivid as the present but can actually evaluate the present by showing its relation, through subconscious associations, with the past. This Bergsonian and Proustian treatment of time was, however, in *Mrs. Dalloway* a means rather than an end. In *To the Lighthouse* it becomes the end itself, for Mrs. Ramsay, in the final section of the book, though dead, lives as vividly in Lily Briscoe's memory as she lived in reality—in fact, more vividly, for the memory of Mrs. Ramsay is for Lily a more powerful experience and a more positively influential one than was Mrs. Ramsay in real life.

But while it is true that *To the Lighthouse* succeeds, through the ever living personality of Mrs. Ramsay, in destroying the tyranny of time, such a comment states only half the truth. For we must ask the same question here that we did with the preceding novel: Who is this Mrs. Ramsay? Petulant critics have complained that Mrs. Ramsay, though one knows she is the wife of a scholar, has a large family of children, spends the summer in the Hebrides, and entertains there a conglomerate house-party, is not flesh and blood. Of course not! She is not intended to be corporeal. She is light; she is spirit; she is an undying (though she dies) spell. She is not Hilda Lessways; she is a luminosity whose rays, like those of dead stars, shine on into eternity. Mrs. Woolf has used the personality of Mrs. Ramsay and the lighthouse itself as symbols of the reality she is trying to portray, a reality that is an intangible and abstract force running through the pattern of life, connecting the past with the present, showing us that

"Toward Virginia Woolf" by *John Hawley Roberts. From* The Virginia Quarterly Review *10, no. 4 (October 1934): 595–97. Copyright 1934* by The Virginia Quarterly Review. *Reprinted by permission of the publisher.*

"nothing is simply one thing." For no object, no event, no point in time is ever static, can ever remain discrete.

A. D. Moody: The Meaning of a Technique

". . . effort, effort, dominates: not the waves: and personality: and defiance. . . ."

Lily Briscoe's "I have had my vision" brings *To the Lighthouse* to a point of rest, of poised wholeness. At the same time the past tense in which she speaks recognises clearly if unemphatically, that it is only an aesthetic resolution that has been achieved. The challenge to the human spirit posed by the natural processes of life has been taken up and answered only in "the other sphere" of art; and the answer, though valid and satisfying so far as it goes, offers no ultimate assurance against "the fertility, the insensibility of nature." "Byzantium," to borrow Yeats' images, does not resolve "the dolphin torn, the gong-tormented sea." The result is that Lily Briscoe's statement, even as it perfects the novel, sets up a faint but disturbing resonance.

In some who lack the author's "negative capability" this has led to an "irritable reaching after fact and certainty": "If only (one finds oneself feeling in reading these novels), if only these dissolved units of understanding had been co-ordinated into a system; if only . . . ; if only . . . , how much safer one would feel." Virginia Woolf knew the value of the sense of safety conferred by systems of thought and behaviour, but she knew too that those are human conventions, not ultimate realities. As an artist her concern was to comprehend the reality as well as the convention—to remember, as it were, that objects we agree for ordinary purposes to regard as solid, are in fact composed of shifting particles. In *To the Lighthouse,* having recognised that in human life there is no ultimate stability or permanence, she had shifted her attention from life to art and stressed such stability and permanence as art could offer. But this obviously was too partial to be fully satisfying. The full implications had still to be faced of the fact that it is not in art that we live, but in the flux of Nature; not in the security of the lighthouse but in the uncontrollable waves.

"The Meaning of a Technique." From Virginia Woolf *by A. D. Moody (Edinburgh: Oliver and Boyd Limited, 1963), pp. 45–46. Reprinted by permission of the publisher.*

Chronology of Important Dates

	Virginia Woolf	The Age
1882	Born January 25.	Gottlieb Daimler builds petrol engine; Leslie Stephen publishes *Science of Ethics*.
1895	Julia Stephen dies.	Freud, *Studien über Hysterie.*
1904	Leslie Stephen dies.	New York, Broadway subway opens.
1905	Virginia Woolf begins publishing.	Einstein's first theory of relativity.
1912	Marriage to Leonard Woolf.	Sinking of *Titanic.*
1914–18	Serious mental breakdown.	World War I.
1915	*Voyage Out.*	*Birth of a Nation,* Einstein's General Theory of Relativity.
1917	Beginning of Hogarth Press.	Eliot, *Prufrock* poems; C. Jung, *The Unconscious;* Bolshevist Revolution.
1919	*Night and Day;* Move to Monk's House.	Versailles Peace Conference; Mussolini founds Italian Fascist Party; Communist 3rd International.
1920		Prohibition in U.S.A.
1922	*Jacob's Room.*	Irish Rebellion; Eliot, *Waste Land;* Joyce, *Ulysses;* Death of Proust.
1924	Move to Tavistock Square.	"Fonofilm" talking pictures.
1925	*Mrs. Dalloway.*	*Mein Kampf.*
1926		Television.

1927	*To the Lighthouse.*	Heisenberg's Uncertainty Principle; Lindbergh's flight; Freud, *Future of an Illusion.*
1928	*Orlando.*	First Mickey Mouse film in color; Yeats, *The Tower;* Graf Zeppelin; Brecht, *Threepenny Opera.*
1931	*The Waves.*	"Frankenstein" with Boris Karloff; Lawrence devises cyclotron.
1936		Spanish Civil War begins; Penguin Books—paperback revolution.
1937	*The Years.*	Skull of Pithecanthropus found in Java; Nazi exhibition of degenerate art in Munich.
1939		German invasion of Poland.
1940	London house bombed.	Einstein: no logical basis for physics.
1941	Death of Virginia Woolf; *Between the Acts* published.	Atomic research begun—"Manhattan Project."
1942	*The Death of the Moth.*	

Notes on the Editor and Contributors

THOMAS A. VOGLER, the editor, is Associate Professor of English Literature and Chairman of the Board of Studies in Literature at the University of California at Santa Cruz. He is the editor of *Twentieth Century Interpretations of Wuthering Heights,* and has published studies of several English and American poets and novelists.

The late ERICH AUERBACH came to the United States in 1947 and joined the faculty of Yale University in 1950, where he became Sterling Professor of Romance Philology in 1956. He wrote extensively on Italian, French and medieval Latin literature. His best known work is *Mimesis: The Representation of Reality in Western Literature.*

DAVID DAICHES is Professor of English at the University of Sussex. He is the author of many articles and works of criticism, including *The Novel and the Modern World.*

The late ELIZABETH DREW was Visiting Lecturer at Smith College for many years and a teacher at the Middlebury College Graduate School of English at Breadloaf. She is the author of *Discovering Poetry, T. S. Eliot: The Design of His Poetry,* and *Poetry, A Modern Guide.*

JEAN GUIGUET is Professor of English at the University of Aix-en-Provence. He is currently working on a French translation of the poetry of Hart Crane.

LODWICK HARTLEY is Professor of English literature and Chairman of the English Department at North Carolina State College. He has published extensively on 18th and 20th Century English literature, including critical studies of William Cowper and Laurence Sterne.

GEOFFREY H. HARTMAN is Professor of English and Comparative Literature at Yale University. Among his publications are *André Malraux* and *Wordsworth's Poetry.*

ARNOLD KETTLE is Senior Lecturer in English at the University of Leeds. He is author of *An Introduction to the English Novel.*

F. R. LEAVIS has written extensively on literature, culture and education. He is one of the founders and past editors of *Scrutiny.* He is currently Honorary Visiting Professor of English at the University of York.

HERMAN MELVILLE is one of the most important American writers of the 19th Century. His works include: *Typee, Omoo, Mardi, Pierre, Moby-Dick,* and *The Confidence Man.*

A. D. MOODY is a member of the English Department at the University of York.

JOSÉ ORTEGA Y GASSET was a Spanish critic and philosopher. Among his best known works are *The Dehumanization of Art* and *The Revolt of the Masses.*

JOHN HAWLEY ROBERTS has taught at the University of Chicago and has published a number of articles and an *Outline Guide to Major English Poets.*

JOSEPHINE O'BRIEN SCHAEFER is Associate Professor of English at Trinity College (D.C.). She is the author of *The Three-Fold Nature of Reality in the Novels of Virginia Woolf.*

Selected Bibliography

For further reading, students should go first to the other works by Virginia Woolf listed below, and to the complete versions of those studies represented in this volume by selections only.

Blackstone, Bernard. *Virginia Woolf, A Commentary.* New York: Harcourt, Brace, 1949 and *Virginia Woolf.* London: British Book Center, 1952. Writers and Their Work series, Vol. 33. Largely a thematic and moralistic approach, sympathetic to its subject but limited by many conventional assumptions about the nature of fiction. Listed here because it received favorable comment from Leonard Woolf.

Blotner, Joseph L. Mythic Pattern in *To the Lighthouse. PMLA* 71, no. 4, pt. 1 (Sept. 1956). A "symbolic" interpretation in which Mrs. Ramsay is "a symbol of the female principle in life." An extreme view of the novel, with some inaccuracies, but suggests many mythic analogues.

Brewster, Dorothy. *Virginia Wolf.* New York: New York University, 1962. Includes a study of Virginia Woolf's criticism and a brief biography as well as a study of the novels.

Friedman, Norman. "The Waters of Annihilation: Double Vision in *To the Lighthouse,*" *English Literary History* 22, I (March 1955).

Forster, E. M. "Virginia Woolf." In Mark Schorer, ed., *Modern British Fiction,* (New York: Oxford University Press, 1961). A general view of Virginia Woolf by a contemporary and novelist with somewhat different views.

Guiguet, Jean. *Virginia Woolf and Her Works.* New York: Harcourt, Brace & World, Inc., 1965. Trans. by Jean Stewart from *Virginia Woolf et Son Oeuvre* (Paris: Didier, 1962). An attempt to study the work and life together in order "to reach the centre, the very core of her being, and that aspect or mode of being which is of particular interest to us: the artist."

Hafley, James. *The Glass Roof.* Berkeley: University of California, 1954. An attempt to trace the continuity and development of Virginia Woolf's oeuvre as a novelist, with general discussions of technique which are helpful for all the novels.

Nathan, Monique. *Virginia Woolf par Elle-même,* ed. du Seuil. Paris: 1956. Available in translation by Herma Briffault: *Virginia Woolf.* New York: Grove Press 1961. A sensitive but impressionistic version of Virginia Woolf's life and work with many quotations and excellent photographs. Not a conventional work, but a very enjoyable one.

Schaefer, Josephine O'Brien. *The Three-Fold Nature of Reality in the Novels of Virginia Woolf.* The Hague: Mouton, 1965. A separate chapter on each of the novels; sees a "faltering" in the work after *The Waves.*

Woolf, Virginia. *A Writer's Diary,* ed. Leonard Woolf. New York: Harcourt, Brace, 1954. Especially for the years 1925–1930.

———. *The Waves.* New York: Harcourt, Brace & Co., 1931. Especially for comparing Bernard's concluding monologue with Lily Briscoe in Part III of *To the Lighthouse.*

———. "Modern Fiction," *Collected Essays,* II. New York: Harcourt, Brace & World, Inc., 1967.

TWENTIETH CENTURY
INTERPRETATIONS

MAYNARD MACK, *Series Editor*
Yale University

NOW AVAILABLE
Collections of Critical Essays
ON

(*continued on next page*)

(continued from previous page)

TWENTIETH CENTURY VIEWS

British Authors

JANE AUSTEN, edited by Ian Watt (S-TC-26)

THE BEOWULF POET, edited by Donald K. Fry (S-TC-82)

BLAKE, edited by Northrop Frye (S-TC-58)

BYRON, edited by Paul West (S-TC-31)

COLERIDGE, edited by Kathleen Coburn (S-TC-70)

CONRAD, edited by Marvin Mudrich (S-TC-53)

DICKENS, edited by Martin Price (S-TC-72)

JOHN DONNE, edited by Helen Gardner (S-TC-19)

DRYDEN, edited by Bernard N. Schilling (S-TC-32)

T. S. ELIOT, edited by Hugh Kenner (S-TC-2)

FIELDING, edited by Ronald Paulson (S-TC-9)

FORSTER, edited by Malcolm Bradbury (S-TC-59)

HARDY, edited by Albert Guérard (S-TC-25)

HOPKINS, edited by Geoffrey H. Hartman (S-TC-57)

A. E. HOUSMAN, edited by Christopher Ricks (S-TC-83)

SAMUEL JOHNSON, edited by Donald J. Greene (S-TC-48)

BEN JONSON, edited by Jonas A. Barish (S-TC-22)

KEATS, edited by Walter Jackson Bate (S-TC-43)

D. H. LAWRENCE, edited by Mark Spilka (S-TC-24)

MARLOWE, edited by Clifford Leech (S-TC-44)

ANDREW MARVELL, edited by George deF. Lord (S-TC-81)

MILTON, edited by Louis L. Martz (S-TC-60)

MODERN BRITISH DRAMATISTS, edited by John Russell Brown (S-TC-74)

RESTORATION DRAMATISTS, edited by Earl Miner (S-TC-64)

SAMUEL RICHARDSON, edited by John Carroll (S-TC-85)